THE MARTIN YEARS:

Norfolk Will Always Remember Roy

BY

Amy Waters Yarsinske

HALLMARK
Publishing Company, Inc.

*T*his book is published under the sponsorship of the Norfolk Historical Society and its Hampton Roads Biography Committee. The biography committee intends that this will be the first in a series of biographical works to portray the lives of important figures in the history of twentieth-century Hampton Roads, a region that cradles the fragile beginnings of the nation's history within its borders.

The author gratefully acknowledges the generosity and support of the Hampton Roads Biography Committee, consisting of James B. Oliver Jr., chairman; Richard F. Barry III, William C. Wooldridge, Louis L. Guy Jr., Thomas G. Johnson Jr., and Vincent J. Mastracco Jr. The committee and the author are deeply appreciative to those whose additional support helped make possible the publication of this series of books: R. Bruce Bradley, Conrad M. Hall, Harry T. Lester, V. H. "Pooch" Nusbaum, Richard D. Roberts, Walter F. Rugaber, Louis F. Ryan, John O. Wynne, and Bleakhorn Foundation. Finally, thanks is extended to the Norfolk Historical Society membership and its officers—James K. Sands, president and treasurer; Helen J. Sonner, vice president; and Charles A. Miller, secretary.

Copyright © 2001 by Amy Waters Yarsinske

B. L. Walton, Jr., *Publisher*
Richard A. Horwege, *Editor*
Rick Vigenski, *Graphic Designer*

Library of Congress Cataloging-in-Publication Data
Yarsinske, Amy Waters, 1963–
     The Martin years : Norfolk will always remember Roy / by Amy Waters Yarsinske.
          p. cm.
     Includes bibliographical references (p.) and index.
     ISBN 1–893276–00–7 (softcover : alk. paper)
     1. Martin, Roy B. 2. Mayors—Virginia—Norfolk—Biography. 3. City council members—Virginia—Norfolk—Biography. 4. Norfolk (Va.)—Politics and government—20th century.   I. Title.
   F234.N8 Y36 2001
   975.5' 521043'092—dc21
                                                          00–054259

Printed in the United States of America

CONTENTS

A little over a year ago, in 1999, Roy B. Martin Jr., former Norfolk mayor and one of the city's greatest boosters in the post–World War II years, decided it was time to document his years of civic leadership in what he figured would be a small tribute piece relegated to an inconspicuous library shelf. He was wrong. Spearheaded by a determined and committed handful of Norfolk leaders, Martin's recollections were destined to come to life on the pages of this book so that the memories and historic record as Roy Martin saw it would become as well read as they were documented in his many scrapbooks, newspaper clippings and, perhaps most importantly—his recollections.

The Martin years reflect Norfolk in a state of transition unlike any other time in the city's history and a young naval officer returning home from the war who was soon to find it rife for change and growth. Norfolk's native son had grown up watching his father build a successful marine supply business. He attended the city's public schools and graduated from Maury High School in 1939. After a year at the Norfolk Division of the College of William and Mary, young Roy Martin earned a bachelor of science degree in commerce from the University of Virginia, graduating with the class of 1943.

After college, with World War II waging in Europe and the Pacific, Roy joined the United States Navy, where he soon attained the rank of lieutenant and was placed in charge of a tank landing ship in the Pacific. Even after the war was over, he remained active in the naval reserves and joined the Matthew Fontaine Maury American Legion Post 300, where he became commander in 1948, the same year he wed the former

As a young Navy lieutenant, Roy Martin served aboard LST 124 in the South Pacific in 1944. His tank landing ship is behind Martin in the photograph. The LST 124 was part of the unnamed LST 1-class. Tank landing ships had their combat debut in the Solomons in June of 1943, and remained in the Pacific theater until cessation of hostilities in August 1945. A remarkably versatile platform, the LST also proved itself able to take a great deal of punishment and survive. There were some 1,051 built during the Second World War, but when they were no longer needed after the fighting stopped, hundreds were either scrapped or sunk.

Martin, standing center, was commander of the Matthew Fontaine Maury Post 300 of the American Legion, succeeding Pryor Wormington, a local attorney, in June of 1948, when this picture was taken of post members erecting a Quonset hut on the beach off Shore Drive at Virginia Beach. The post was composed entirely of veterans of World War II and primarily from Norfolk. Other officers elected at the time Martin was installed as commander were J. Lamar Davis, first vice commander; James B. Richardson, second vice commander; Richard Burnette, adjutant; John W. Winston Jr., finance; Thomas M. Johnston, sergeant-at-arms; Spencer G. Gill Jr., chaplain; and Toy D. Savage, historian. Martin remained active in the naval reserves at this time. (Photo Craftsmen, Inc.)

Louise Freeman Eggleston. She would remain a stalwart supporter and life partner to Roy and, in so many respects, the driving force behind his success in public life and private business.

To make a living on his return to Norfolk, Roy started a business called Kay-Mar Clothes, Inc., which was charted in October of 1946 for the manufacture of dress trousers. His partner in the venture, James H. Kabler, had been a classmate at the University of Virginia and both served in the Navy during the war. "We came back from the war thinking we could do anything and became involved in many things," he would later recall. Kay-Mar was located at 15–17 Roanoke Avenue and expected, upon getting operational, to manufacture twenty-five hundred pairs of trousers a week. Perhaps the young partners were overly optimistic because the business folded in less than two years, but Roy soon found employment with Foote Brothers and Company (later Commonwealth Food Brokerage, Inc.), a food brokerage concern located on Water Street, a short distance from his former clothing plant on Roanoke Avenue. The Foote brothers, George and Gaston, brought Roy into the company and it was there he found his niche in the bustling commerce then on Norfolk's waterfront.

When Roy came home to Norfolk, the city bristled with sailors and soldiers, roustabouts, and transients who frequented the liquor and burlesque houses that had given Norfolk its honky-tonk reputation in the war years. While the city was busy, its quality of life and the character of its once beautiful downtown had been diminished by the spate of activities that would later lead Martin and members of the city council to declare redevelopment a godsend.

Roy Martin was a thirty-two-year-old father of two young children when he was first brought onto the Norfolk City Council to fill the term of James M. Williams, who resigned on September 1, 1953. Roy became the youngest member of what would be dubbed the "businessman's council." He would recall in later years what a risk he took taking a city council seat, his life full of the ups and downs of raising children and nurturing a blossoming career at the food brokerage house he would later own.

The strength of Martin's tenure on city council, which endured for twenty-one years, twelve of them as mayor, had its roots in the strong power structure in Norfolk that brought the city together after World War II. The business community, disenchanted with Norfolk's image as a town of backward slums and whorehouses, and sensing economic doom without drastic action, came together behind a reform ticket consisting of prominent businessmen from equally prominent families. The ticket won and the businessman's or silk-stocking council reigned for another quarter century.

When the mantle of power passed to W. (William) Fred Duckworth in 1950, this abrupt, but indefatigable man who made Roy Martin his protégé and bequeathed to him a tradition of strong leadership and bold accomplishment, ran roughshod over his opponents and demanded absolute unanimity from his colleagues, all businessmen supported by business-minded civic leaders. Many of them, like Martin in 1953, came aboard the city council as appointments to fill out terms for councilmen who had either deceased in office or resigned. Although Martin cut his teeth on council this way, so did Linwood F. "Cy" Perkins, later Roy's longtime vice mayor; V. H. "Pooch" Nusbaum Jr., another Martin vice mayor; George S. Hughes; Lewis L. Layton; and Paul T. Schweitzer. Appointments gave these councilmen the opportunity to stand for election as incumbents, a decided advantage over candidates outside either the Duckworth or, later, Martin regime.

The businessmen's councils of Duckworth and Martin literally changed the face of Norfolk, making those bricks-and-mortar changes that rebuilt a lagging downtown and replaced slums with public housing, opened new highways and thoroughfares throughout and around the city, and brought substantial federal

A fiftieth reunion of the Thomas Jefferson Society and the University of Virginia class of 1943 was held May 18–19, 1993, in Charlottesville. Roy Martin received a bachelor of science degree in commerce from the University, which he attended from 1940 through 1943. Due to the war, Martin's degree program was accelerated one year and he finished in three years instead of the standard four. Here, members of the society and class of 1943 stand on the steps of the Rotunda. (University of Virginia Alumni Association photograph.)

funding to bear on social and economic inequities that permeated Norfolk, the principal city on Hampton Roads' south side. The failings of Duckworth and Martin as mayors, in retrospect, have focused on their often abrupt approach to dealing with citizens and—at times—one another. Many who admired the council's achievements in this era of businessman's government were often put off quickly by the council's swift rebuke of any opposition or criticism. The end of the regime of Duckworth and Martin came gradually, beginning with Sam T. Barfield's election as an independent to council in 1960, and two years earlier if one vote against public school closure can be traced to the collapse of unanimity that Duckworth so enjoyed as president of the council for over a decade. There would be more independents and issues to come, such as Robert E. Summers' break with the Martin council and reelection to office as an independent in 1966 or black Civil Rights attorney Joseph A. Jordan Jr.'s ascent to city council two years later, but in the end, it would be a collective majority that overruled the Martin era, yet not his spirit. Despite losing his majority hold on city council in 1972, Roy would continue to conduct his meetings with the brusqueness for which he was so well known.

"Many will regret his departure," wrote *Ledger-Star* political writer Tom Reilly, on April 15, 1974, "many will hail it—the Martin of Norfolk's 'Martin Years.'" Roy himself would remark of his eminent departure, "sure, there have been disappointments and, I believe, accomplishments, but I have no regrets nor apologies about actions I have taken." While many will readily recall his often sharp tone in council chambers, Roy also had the kind words to follow when circumstances warranted them. His longtime friend and former vice mayor Pooch Nusbaum once said of Roy: "When he spoke and acted, he didn't have the next election in mind in regard to himself. To me, he has placed the best interests of the people of Norfolk above everything else—and at great risk to himself."[1] Standing accused of focusing more on bricks and mortar than people's needs, Roy would always retort: "Bricks and mortar create jobs, during construction and operation afterwards. Bricks and mortar provide facilities for use of people,"[2] and he was right. And of the man who raised him in the politics of post–World War II Norfolk, Roy said many years later that outside of his own father, "I don't know of anybody who influenced my development more than Fred Duckworth, and I'm not ashamed to say it."

The story of Roy Martin's civic and political contributions to his city and the region is as honest as his memory serves and the record shows. He wanted, more than anything else, for the story to be complete as space would allow, and it was with this in mind that records from the Norfolk City Council; the Norfolk newspapers; Roy's voluminous scrapbooks, paper and photographic archives—and memory—were drawn upon to complete his biography.

Since this is the most appropriate place as any to say so, it may be duly noted here what one *Virginian-Pilot* editorial writer observed over a quarter century ago. Roy Martin has earned the casual eminence of "first-name recognition." Accordingly, "it is enough to mention 'Roy' as it is enough to say 'Henry' (Henry H. Howell Jr.) or 'Mills' (Mills E. Godwin Jr.) or 'Sidney' (Sidney S. Kellam)."[3] To

Roy, who once quipped that his life had always been in the hands of women, read on. Of the three women Roy has observed are the most important in his life, one is a relative newcomer. Louise, his devoted and wonderful wife of over a half-century, is the one person Roy has said repetitively is "the light of his life." Then there is Sue Coupe, his longtime secretary, whom Roy has noted "kept me going on task and in the right direction day after day." And now, perhaps the most humbly of all, Roy said to this author as I left his house the last time, loaded for bear with photographs and memory books, "my life is in your hands now." I dedicate your life's story, Roy, to Louise, your lovely bride and life partner. She earned the title of "Mrs. Mayor" alongside you all those years. She was a capable and gracious ambassador for the city of Norfolk. Without her devotion to you and your children, Roy B. Martin III and Anne Martin Sessoms, the career you enjoyed in public life and business, as you have said, "could not have happened," nor been so successful. In the end, Louise's meticulously kept record of Roy's tenure as a Norfolk city councilman—and mayor—made this book possible. Thank you, Mrs. Mayor.

Politically active after World War II, Roy Martin was often in the company of the group shown here circa 1948. (Left to right) Martin, James E. "Jim" Barry, Congressman Porter Hardy Jr., Samuel R. Sargeant, and Harry B. Vesey Jr. are pictured at a political get-together sponsored by the Second District Democratic Committee for U.S. Senator A. Willis Robertson and Hardy, both of whom drew active support from Norfolk's younger voters for their reelection bids. (Photo Craftsmen, Inc.)

CHAPTER 1

Putting Political Activism to Practice

In 1948, the city of Norfolk elected the Cooke-Darden-Twohy ticket to city council and began what turned out to be almost thirty years of "businessman's government." This ticket was made up of Richard D. Cooke, a well-known Norfolk attorney; Pretlow Darden, an automobile dealer; and John Twohy II, a prominent businessman. They agreed to serve only one term, but that one term set the course of Norfolk from 1948 to September 1974.

Under the Cooke-Darden-Twohy team, a new city manager, C. A. Harrell, was brought into Norfolk. Harrell began his almost five-year tenure in November of 1946 with the full support of the Cooke-Darden-Twohy councilmanic ticket of progressive city government. He served until December 1951 when Henry H. George III again became acting city manager until his permanent appointment to the job on September 2, 1952. During the Cooke-Darden-Twohy years, a business-type pro-

A paid political advertisement in The Virginian-Pilot *from June of 1949 featured five prominent Young Democratic Club members set to speak on behalf of State Senator John S. Battle, a candidate for governor. Battle won the election and served as Virginia's governor from 1950 to 1954. A committee of nine young men and women, of whom Martin was one, made Battle's win of the Second Congressional District possible. Other members of the committee included Mary Cary Willcox Johnston (Mrs. Thomas M.), Allen Reynolds, Archie L. Boswell, Richard B. Spindle III, John F. "Jack" Rixey, Irvine B. Hill, Crenshaw Reed, and Grace Lee Butler.*

Democratic U.S. Senator Harry Flood Byrd, of Virginia, (pictured here center) was running for reelection in 1952 when he came to the city for a breakfast meeting sponsored by the young men's committee of the Norfolk Byrd-for-Senate Committee. Roy B. Martin Jr. was chairman of the young men's committee. Martin's fellow committee members, shown in the photograph left to right, were H. Singleton Garrett, O. Ray Yates, Senator Byrd, James E. "Jim" Barry, Martin, and J. Warren White Jr. At the time the picture was taken, O. Ray Yates was president of the Norfolk Young Democratic Club and Warren White served as president of the state organization with Jim Barry sitting as chairman of the Second Congressional District. Martin succeeded Yates as president of the Young Democratic Club on June 12, 1953. (Photo Craftsmen, Inc.)

Roy B. Martin Jr., newly appointed Norfolk city councilman, posed with his wife, Louise, and the couple's two children: Anne Beverly, eight months (on her mother's lap) and Roy B. "Sandy" Martin III, three-and-a-half. The photograph ran in The Ledger-Dispatch *on September 16, 1953.*

Members of the Norfolk City Council and other city officials confer with members of Norfolk's delegation to the 1954 Virginia General Assembly on November 30, 1953. Left to right: Delegate Lawrence C. Page, Mayor W. Fred Duckworth, Councilman N. B. Etheridge, City Attorney Jonathan W. Old, Delegate Delamater Davis, Delegate Theodore C. Pilcher, City Manager H. H. George III, Assistant City Attorney Leighton P. Roper, Delegate John F. "Jack" Rixey, Delegate Toy D. Savage Jr., Delegate Walter A. Page, State Senator Robert F. Baldwin Jr., Delegate James W. Roberts, Councilman Roy B. Martin Jr., Councilman Robert F. Ripley, and Vice Mayor George R. Abbott. The photograph originally ran in the December 1, 1953 edition of The Norfolk Virginian-Pilot.

gram was brought into the city, a plan that directly reflected on the choice of Harrell as city manager and his successor, Henry George. "[It was] not politics as usual," Martin is quick to point out. "During these four years, Dick Cooke served for two years as mayor and Pretlow Darden served as mayor for the last two years. It was during this time that Norfolk Redevelopment and Housing Authority began to become a real force in the future development of Norfolk. I used to always say that it was this team that tilled the ground for the future. The team led by W. Fred Duckworth planted the seeds and the Martin team had the opportunity and the privilege of beginning to bring in the crops."

In 1952, with the Cooke-Darden-Twohy team, standing by their word not to serve but one term, relinquished their seats on the city council to new blood. A ticket of W. Fred Duckworth, Robert F. Ripley, James M. Williams, and N. B. Etheridge took control of city council in the election that followed. This ticket had the full support of not only the Cooke-Darden-Twohy team, but also the majority of the Norfolk business community. The newly formed council elected Duckworth mayor, a position he held for the next twelve years. Duckworth had been with the Ford Motor Company before the war as its Charlotte, North Carolina manager and dur-

ing the war, with the United States government's War Production Board. "Bob Ripley was a young, well-known owner of a successful real-estate and insurance business. Williams was manager of a local life insurance company and Etheridge owned a downtown parking garage along with other properties," recalled Martin, "but in 1953, the unexpected happened. Williams resigned from the city council for personal reasons, thereby creating a vacancy, which under the Norfolk city charter would be filled until the next council election." The next election was scheduled for June 8, 1954, creating what was later to be a game of musical chairs to determine who would get a council seat.

A search of nearly two weeks ensued to find a man to fill Williams' seat on the Norfolk City Council. The search ended with the selection of Roy Martin, then a thirty-two-year-old food broker who had been active in civic and political affairs since the close of World War II. "On the afternoon of September 1, 1953, I received a call at my office, which was then Foote Brothers and Company (later to become Commonwealth Food Brokerage, Inc.) from Bob Ripley who didn't ask, but told me to come to the mayor's office in City Hall at once. I recall telling Bob I couldn't leave right away, but that 'I'd be there just as soon as possible.' He hung up on me before I could say anything further."

"I walked to City Hall since my office was not very far away." When he arrived, Martin found all of the members of the council gathered there—Mayor Duckworth, Vice Mayor George R. Abbott, and Councilmen Robert F. Ripley, Ezra T. Summers, Lawrence C. Page, and N. B. Etheridge. "After a few words of greeting, Duckworth got right to the point. He told me the council was interested in filling the vacancy with a young businessman and my name had been suggested." Asked how he would feel about being a member of the council, Martin reacted with surprise. However, since he had been active in both civic and political affairs, the soon-to-be council-man responded that it would be "very interesting, challenging and an honor." Mayor Duckworth then asked if any other member of council had any questions of Martin to which there were a few about his background as well as some of Roy's civic and political activities. Then Duckworth made the offer which would thrust Roy Martin onto the center stage of city politics, asking bluntly: "Would you accept this appointment?" Martin hesitated, replying he was honored but would need to talk with George Foote, then president of Foote Brothers and Company, when he returned from vacation the following Monday. "Without a moment for further comment from me, the mayor interjected: 'Roy, if you want to be a mem-ber of this council, you must be prepared to make decisions and act quickly. Do you want it or not?'" Pressed for an answer, Roy made one of the most important decisions of his life. In answer to Mayor Duckworth's hard-put demand to ante up, he replied, "'Yes, Mr. Mayor, I would like the appointment.'" Thus began twenty-one years of interesting, sometimes difficult, but mostly rewarding years of his life. "Little did I know that day what a difference this answer made to the future years of my life." Martin was elected by the council at their following Tuesday council meeting. The date was September 22, 1953.

Over forty-five years later, Roy Martin would remark that accepting his first city council seat was extraordinary given the fact he was so young, "and let's not forget married with a three-year-old son and a nine-month-old daughter. I realize what a gamble I took." Fortunately for a gregarious young businessman, his employer—George Foote—had himself been active in Norfolk civic affairs as a member of the Norfolk Port Authority and his brother, Gaston, had been chair-man of the Portsmouth School Board. Upon George Foote's return to Norfolk, his only comment to Roy was: "Continue to do a good job for Foote Brothers and Company, while at the same time, do your best to help make Norfolk a better city for all its citizens."

Among the first issues to pique Martin's attention as city council's newest—and youngest—member was the increasing rate of juvenile delinquency in Norfolk. At the council meeting on November 19, 1953, Roy noted that juvenile delin-quency in the city of Norfolk was up considerably from the previous year. "This was my first attempt to bring before council a matter not already on the docket," he recalled recently, "and in December of that year, a study committee made up of a number of prominent people, was appointed to provide a report to council." The report related unmistakably that the public schools were best suited to cope with the problem with, of course, the proper support from city government, including the police department and the courts system. The sixty-six-page finding laid out numerous points and recommendations based on the 1953 police and court records while also outlining attempts and steps that should be taken to curtail this pervasive problem. "Unfortunately, when we look back to 1953 and fast-forward to now—1999—we find that the problem still exists and has possibly gotten more violent because in those days we didn't have schoolchildren bringing guns to school."

VOTE TOMORROW

and Give These Candidates a Justly Deserved

VOTE OF CONFIDENCE

W. FRED DUCKWORTH

N. B. ETHERIDGE

LAWRENCE C. PAGE

Vote

Tomorrow

Polls Open
6:30 a. m.
to 7:30 p. m.

ROY B. MARTIN, JR.

ROBERT F. RIPLEY

Vote

Tomorrow

Polls Open
6:30 a. m.
to 7:30 p. m.

Service on Norfolk's City Council is a demanding and often tedious task. It has slight reward, but is a fine opportunity for service to one's city. One has only his recompense, the satisfaction of a job well done and the appreciation of his fellow citizens. The most concrete way we, as citizens, can show our appreciation is by expressing it at the polls tomorrow. Norfolk is infamous throughout the State for the laxity of its voters. Maybe it is because we have a City governed by honest and able men. However, the repercussions of a small vote can be many and varied. It is first, of course, discouraging to these

men who have served you so faithfully and well. It makes it difficult to get the most talented citizens to take part in public life. It broadcasts to the State and the Nation that we have only a slight interest in preserving our freedoms and our way of life.

Tomorrow let each voter make it his responsibility to change Norfolk's reputation and take the few minutes necessary to VOTE and give a Vote of Confidence to Messrs. DUCKWORTH, ETHERIDGE, MARTIN, PAGE and RIPLEY.

These candidates pledge...

...to continue to promote and maintain the same high level of services to the community that has been evidenced in the past four years. In brief, they will do their utmost to further promote the City's physical improvement, its health, its welfare, its safety and its opportunity for cultural and recreational growth.

This ad sponsored by the following members of the Councilmanic Campaign Committee:

This advertisement ran in the June 7, 1954 Virginian-Pilot. Five incumbent councilmen, including Roy, were reelected the following day.

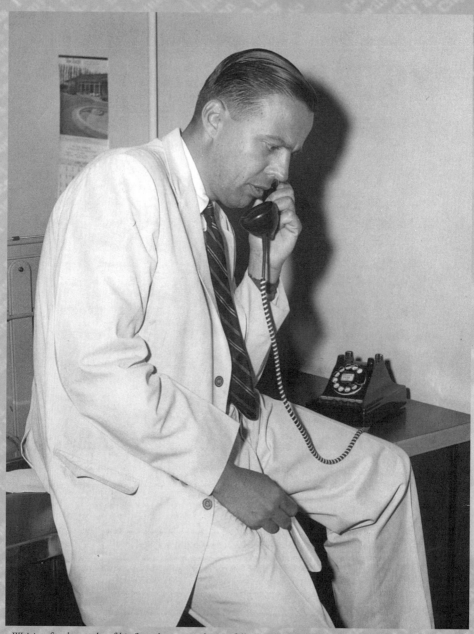

Waiting for the results of his first election to the Norfolk City Council, Roy B. Martin remained close to the telephone on the evening of June 8, 1954. (John Pilling, photographer.)

The Missing Seventh Member:
Roy's First Election
to Council

A vacancy developed suddenly—and without precedent—on Norfolk's new seven-member city council within a day of the June 8, 1954 election. The situation arose when Councilman Robert F. Ripley formally qualified for the seat he won in the municipal election. But Ripley's qualification was not the end of the problem; it was only the start of an uncomfortable process that left newly elected councilman Roy Martin temporarily without a seat on the council.

Events leading up to June 8 unfolded as follows: James M. Williams, elected to office in 1952 to a four-year term, resigned and the council appointed Martin to fill the vacancy until the next election. Martin opted to run for a full four-year term in that election, but when the votes were tallied, while Roy had won a seat beginning September 1, it was Ripley, whose existing seat on council did not expire until August 30, who was elected to serve out the remainder of Williams' original term. Ripley was administered the oath of office as successor to Williams by Clerk of the Corporation Court William L. Prieur Jr. on June 10, but it left a two-month vacancy on Ripley's original term of office. Martin, at least for a short time, was without a council seat.

The city council immediately met to resolve the issue of Martin as the odd man out. Ripley was recognized at the following Tuesday council meeting as Williams' elected successor. The six councilmen, including Ripley, then appointed Martin to fill Ripley's unexpired term. Martin qualified immediately and began serving out Ripley's two-month gap until his own four-year term started on the first of September. He did not even miss a meeting of the city council.

In certifying the vote, commissioners of the election certified the voter turnout at 5,284, 48 less voters than the unofficial total compiled on election night, but perhaps most importantly, the order of finish in the election did not change. Councilman N. B. Etheridge came in first with 4,446 votes; Martin, 4,364; Page, 4,251; Mayor W. Fred Duckworth, 4,171; and Ripley, 4,144. Drewry Little, the losing candidate, was credited with 2,191 votes. Ripley's last-place finish among incumbent councilmen in an at-large election dictated that he qualified for Williams' remaining two years and not a full four-year seat on city council. The voter turnout was generally considered, at that time, the lowest on record in Norfolk since the outbreak of World War II. The significance of a low turnout meant that referendums on disputed council actions over the next two years could be forced on petition of 1,321 qualified voters—an extraordinarily low figure that would soon reverberate back to a city council already casting

Lee Ann Meriwether—Miss America 1954 and a native of Los Angeles—visited Norfolk on her national postwin tour. She is shown here with Ben Wahrman, convention bureau director of the Norfolk Chamber of Commerce (right), and City Councilman Roy Martin, sent to greet her on behalf of Norfolk's leadership. Meriwether made her appearance at the Suburban Appliance Company, located in the city's Ward's Corner business district. Suburban Appliance, a Philco distributor, was owned by Sidney Edelstein and it was Edelstein's initiative that brought Miss America to Norfolk. (William McIntosh, photographer. McIntosh Studios.)

aspersions on the number and their fear that voters would turn against controversial initiatives too quickly by referendum.

The council's musical chairs maneuvering was soon followed by a July 1954 referendum harking back to the reelection of incumbents Mayor Duckworth and Councilmen Etheridge and Ripley and the first election win by Martin. Each had been returned to office by a very small voter turnout. This left *The Ledger-Dispatch*, the city's evening newspaper, to conclude that Duckworth's council would likely face a referendum to determine the validity of votes cast in the previous month's election. The reason for the referendum was far from simple. A referendum could be called on a petition carrying the signatures of qualified voters equal to 25 percent of the vote cast in the last council electoral process. The council election of June 8, with only 5,322 votes, meant that the requirements of only 1,331 signatures would force the council to put the matter in question before voters—again. "This turned out to be the case in 1955 when there was a referendum on the sale of the Norfolk City Market," remarked Martin. "However, the vote did uphold the city council position on the sale of this property."

Following the reorganizational meeting of the city council as dictated by Norfolk's charter, on September 1, 1954, Mayor Duckworth was reappointed president of the council by his colleagues. An editorial in the following day's *Virginian-Pilot* observed that if the city's populace thought local government was any less complicated than state or federal governance, think again. "Four months from now, this council will acquire jurisdiction over 50,000 more people and 11 more square miles in what is now the Tanner's Creek District of Norfolk County. On January 1, the council will have jurisdiction over a city estimated by some officials as having 288,000 people and fifty square miles, with as many problems per square mile as any city in Virginia."

When the council was reorganized in 1952 with a membership increase from five to seven city councilmen, the newspapers noted that perhaps a significant phase of the city's history was about to unfold. The press could not have been more accurate in its pronouncement. With the buzzwords *referendum* and *annexation* swirling around Norfolk City Hall, anxiety and anticipation preyed on the minds of the council as the summer of 1955 entered its dog days. A Norfolk citizens committee had formed to force a referendum on the targeted annexation of forty-one acres of Princess Anne County east of the city of Norfolk's existing corporate boundary. The committee had allied itself with political interests in the county, sparking a wide debate over the personal reasons for Norfolk citizens involving themselves in a Princess Anne County matter. The Norfolk City Council, in response to the committee's establishment of a $50,000 antiannexation fund, increased its own annexation fund by the same and called upon City Manager Henry H. George III to investigate the referendum petition and step up studies of engineering studies to determine the square miles the city could afford to cede under annexation. In the meantime, it was readily apparent that the leaders of the failed referendum bid to stop the sale of the City Market—Reynolds M. Wilkinson Jr. and Floyd R. Pledger—had become the prospective heads of the Norfolk antiannexation committee. Martin was immediately suspect of their personal motives and alarmed at the misinformation on the annexation plan being floated around the city by the antiannexation committee. In a comment to the press after a council meeting, Martin remarked: "Whether we will ask for two miles or forty-one miles, we cannot determine all the factors until our engineers have made their complete reports." Playing upon what a *Virginian-Pilot* editorial dubbed "the weakness of a badly tipped playing hand," Martin moved to protect the facts—and the city council's record of opening the door to the city's future growth through annexation, the Tanner's Creek annexation being the example most touted at the time.

The antiannexation referendum was only symptomatic of a more vexing problem for city fathers. The door to petitions for referendums was swung wide open by low voter turnout in the 1954 election and it was not going to close until city council looked hard at charter changes. Martin moved for review of Section 35 (the referendum clause) of the city charter as petitions to force a second special election were being received by city council. The petitions, bearing the signatures of 2,488 registered voters, were the result of a forty-hour whirlwind petition drive carried out by black property owners in the Broad Creek Shores section of the city, located near Ingleside Elementary School. An ordinance to condemn a forty-three-acre tract for school and park uses was halted by the petitions, truncating the school's further development and pulling a soft use—a park—from the neighborhood. The time had come, said Martin, "to ask the Virginia legislature for some changes."

The term *referendum* clung to the city council's weekly docket like no other issue in 1955. The council had asked the city manager to study what charter changes could be made and recommended to them with regard to referendums. The request was brought about not only by the attempt to call for a referendum on Norfolk's annexation on the Tanner's Creek area of Norfolk County, but came up shortly thereafter when the city of Norfolk was again discussing annexation of Princess Anne County. Before the city council could decide the precise boundary of the land in the county it wished to annex, "referendum again rose its ugly head. Fortunately, it did not prevail and the city of Norfolk did request an annexation of an area of approximately thirty-three square miles of Princess Anne County," noted Martin recently, "but it was going to be a tough sell to the state judiciary." The city-county discussion pertaining to annexation was tenuous at best because Princess Anne County openly opposed such a move by Norfolk and the city, which was bursting at the seams, needed to expand its land area. At one point, Norfolk's attorneys optimistically presented council with their view of the state court's potential ruling on the city's annexation request. "They felt strongly the courts would probably give the city of Norfolk more land than it had requested but, unfortunately, this did not prove to be the case," Martin recalled many years later.

The personal—and political—rift between former Norfolk State Delegate W. Carl Spencer and Martin took no prisoners, the councilman openly accusing the delegate of causing a behind-the-scenes upheaval in the future growth of the city "just to keep his name in the newspapers," by claiming he would be running in the next council election on an antiannexation platform. The delegate sharply retorted, noting that he knew the annexation was wrong, "no one knows how much it will cost, and in voting for it the [city council] bought a pig in a poke." Spencer continued to accuse the city council of being "afraid of the public voice," and his persistent claim that cost should be determined before more land was acquired never let up. Whether the exchanges between the city council and Spencer, part of the public record, were a factor in the state court's eventual decision is indeterminable. Martin said at the time: "Why not let the three learned judges who will make up the court, and not the politicians, decide if annexation is good or bad for the city of Norfolk."

The final decision on annexation between the city of Norfolk and Princess Anne County was made by a three-judge panel—an arrangement that had been changed a few years prior to Norfolk's 1955 entreaty for more land by the Virginia General Assembly. The panel initially consisted of a judge from the annexed area, a judge from the annexing area, and an independent judge appointed by the State Court.

The Norfolk City Council, photographed by Virginian-Pilot *photographer Charles S. Borjes during their organizational meeting on September 1, 1954, consisted of (left to right): Roy B. Martin Jr., Ezra T. Summers, George R. Abbott, Mayor W. Fred Duckworth, Lawrence C. Page, Robert L. Ripley, and N. B. Etheridge.*

Under the subsequent change, the annexed area had one judge, the annexing area did not have a judge and rather than one, there were two independent judges on the panel. "Much to our surprise—and disappointment—the three-judge panel came back recommending an area of just 13.5 square miles. The reason offered by the court noted that the boundary lines the city had asked for would include what is now the Princess Anne High School and also would have absorbed the Little Creek ferry complex, which the judge's panel determined was the only rail line that came into that area."

"The curtailment of the city's growth through annexation was a great setback for Norfolk because we badly needed the land for industrial development and other businesses which keep a thriving community moving forward. One of the real problems that we find even today is that Virginia remains the only state in the Union that does not have city-county shared government," Martin aptly pointed out. The cities are independent and the counties are independent by law. States with shared city and county governance have the capacity to control such important services as their school systems and expansion of a city into a surrounding county. Likewise, Virginia still controls what taxes cities and counties can impose on their residents under the Dillon Rule. "As my good friend, the late State Delegate J. Warren White, used to tell me, "[Virginia's] cities are just wards of the state government."

As Roy settled into his role on Norfolk City Council, he observed the workings of a city government in many respects exceeding that of the average American municipality. Sherwood Reeder, who had been city manager in the city of Richmond, became Norfolk's new manager on July 18, 1955, replacing former public works director and City Manager Henry H. George III. Reeder came to Norfolk as a man with a message, espousing the tenets of good government that Norfolk officials needed to hear, namely that "there must be a maximum of cooperation among governments within a metropolitan area such as we have here." Reeder came upon the

Norfolk political scene much as Roy did—mid-stream—and at a time when the city was beginning a new chapter of history from which much was expected and much later came. "Reeder proved to be an excellent manager during his brief time of less than a year in office. Sadly, he died suddenly while helping dedicate the opening of a skating rink in the Twenty-first Street area of the city." He was then followed by Thomas F. Maxwell who served as city manager for twelve years.

Not all the issues before Norfolk City Council pertained to the prickly issues of annexation or referendums. Some of the most interesting, at least in retrospect, held regional interest then and now. In September of 1956, Norfolk inserted itself in the middle of a bid by the communities of Warwick, Newport News, and Hampton to be enjoined as the city of Hampton Roads, opposing the consolidation with a resolution, submitted by Roy Martin, charging that the use of the name would be misleading and cause undue problems to the port of Norfolk. History was on Norfolk's side in the disagreement that ensued. The name *Hampton Roads* had been used since the first settlers passed through the body of water to which the name refers in the early 1600s. The term had been applied to the port communities in general by the mid-1950s, thus sparking Norfolk's move to block any one community from taking the name *Hampton Roads* for themselves. The consolidation was defeated in a referendum, ending the matter for the time being, but it certainly elicited a flurry of public opinion and alarm on the part of Norfolk politicians and citizens. The late Louis Guy, a member of the House of Delegates from Norfolk, introduced a bill to prohibit the use of *Hampton Roads* as the name of any city in Virginia. The bill passed the House and was rejected by the Senate after intense debate. Guy's bill went a long way toward edifying the people of Virginia as to the name and what it is—a broad deep channel or roadstead which connects the estuary of the James River with the Chesapeake Bay; and is also a part of the estuary which is at the convergence of the James, Elizabeth, and Nansemond Rivers. All of the cities of Hampton Roads share a proprietary interest in this roadstead's name.

On a positive note, the city council moved forward with plans to develop the 2,600-acre Broad Creek Village public housing tract as an industrial park. The city's move was made largely in recognition of the fact that a significant number of cities all over the United States were aggressively seeking new industries and business activities as well as trying to curry favor among their existing industries with financial enticements to stay or expand operations. The city of Norfolk made provision for industrial growth and expansion by purchasing the Broad Creek tract from the federal government through the Norfolk Redevelopment and Housing Authority.

On January 30, 1956, the city agreed to purchase the Broad Creek Village land—now called the Norfolk Industrial Park—for a total of $1.182 million, less any income received from the operation of the project by the Authority. City Ordinance No.18078 approved the agreement between the Norfolk Redevelopment and Housing Authority and the city of Norfolk to the purchase of the land for the agreed price. The final figure, however, after deduction for operational expenses incurred by the Housing Authority was a little over half a million dollars or $1,085 per acre. During the ten-year development period calculated through December 31, 1967, the city collected real-estate taxes from the properties sold in Norfolk Industrial Park totaling nearly $760,000, a fair return on a worthwhile investment in the economic viability of the city.

Roy Martin was, in many regards, a full-time councilman with a full-time job, which he also ran with great success. At the end of September 1956, Roy bought Foote Brothers and Company, where he had been an associate since 1947. The change of ownership marked the retirement of brothers George A. and Gaston S. Foote from the food brokerage business they had run together since 1922. The firm they passed to their associate served wholesalers throughout eastern North Carolina and the Hampton Roads area, while also handling a large number of major commodity accounts for nationally recognized brand-name foods. Though Martin initially had no plans to change the name of the company, he eventually did so, calling it Commonwealth Food Brokerage, Inc.

In the midst of the continuing debate over annexation and the intense planning that accompanied projects such as Norfolk's first industrial park complex and a downtown civic center, Councilman Ezra T. Summers died suddenly in June of 1957 and was replaced by Linwood F. "Cy" Perkins, a prominent local businessman who later served as vice mayor (1962–1970) for the first eight years that Martin was mayor. The loss of Summers on the council was a personal one for his colleagues, many of whom had come up in Norfolk politics during Summers' era.

"... Why should he (Spencer) try to cause such an upheaval in the future growth of our city just to keep his name in the newspapers ..."

So spoke Councilman Roy B. Martin, Jr., at Council yesterday.

"I know this annexation is wrong, no one knows how much it will cost, and in voting for it the Council bought a pig in a poke."

So said W. Carl Spencer last week after he announced that he would actively oppose the annexation plan.

W. Carl Spencer, a former member of the Virginia House of Delegates, was a constant critic of the Duckworth administration, openly opposing the council's annexation plans and often challenging a young city councilman named Roy Martin to terse exchanges during weekly council meetings. Spencer's photograph, which appeared alongside Martin's in a September 15, 1955 Virginian-Pilot article titled, "Spencer Endangers Future of Norfolk, Martin Claims," was an articulate and well-informed spokesman to the issues of the day.

TONIGHT on 2 Stations

6:15 WTAR-TV CHANNEL 3

8:30 WAVY-TV CHANNEL 10

Charles L. Kaufman
Paul G. Caplan
Ben J. Willis
Col. James W. Roberts

Speaking in behalf of and urging you to vote for . . .

- ☒ W. F. DUCKWORTH
- ☒ L. C. PAGE
- ☒ N. B. ETHERIDGE
- ☒ ROY B. MARTIN, JR.
- ☒ LINWOOD F. PERKINS

VOTE TOMORROW
and Return these men to Norfolk City Council

Duckworth, Page, Etheridge, Martin, Perkins
Campaign Committee

The paid political advertisement that ran on June 9, the day before the election in 1958, touted four prominent speakers on behalf of the Duckworth ticket.

CHAPTER 3

One Vote

Five of Norfolk's incumbent city councilmen, including Mayor W. Fred Duckworth, announced their bid for reelection on January 25, 1958. Among those who vowed to continue working on behalf of "sound progressive government" and to continue to bring into reality a far-reaching program of improvements which were then in what many considered their crucial early stages of development stood Duckworth, N. B. Etheridge, Lawrence C. Page, Linwood F. "Cy" Perkins, and Roy Martin. Duckworth, mayor since 1950, was considered the proverbial spark plug of administration efforts to bring Norfolk into its own. Alongside him were longtime friends and political allies Etheridge and Page, both of whom began their tenure on city council with the mayor. Four of the five seats up for election in June 1958 were for full four-year terms. The seat held by Perkins was for the remaining two years on Ezra Summers' term. Election rules were then structured such that the five candidates for reelection ran at large and the one with the least votes would serve out Summers' remaining two-year term. Opposing the incumbents were Drewry Little, Louis Francis Everett, and Floyd R. Pledger, all running as independents.

The opposition was a vocal lot on subjects they vehemently opposed. Critical of downtown redevelopment, they charged the city council with ignoring the interests of Ocean View, Pledger and Little's district. But the charges, such that they were, never found a strong enough audience among voters. After the voting was complete, all of the incumbents were returned to council and the independents went home in defeat. On the positive side, voter turnout was up to 8,129, a far cry better than previous elections.

Norfolk enjoyed longevity in its mayors and city councilmen in those days. The four years spanning 1958 to 1962 were expected to be critical in the history—and future—of the city. Norfolk was putting on a new face with downtown redevelopment and could not afford a hiccup at the polls during the 1958 election. The city council as it stood before and after the election consisted of councilmen sympathetic to the development plans in store for Norfolk's coming of age just as they had been to the myriad of issues that had only recently become hot buttons during the election: annexation, highway widening, port development, a regional airport, and new industrial park.

you owe it to yourself

For Your Best Interest . . .
SUPPORT GOOD
GOVERNMENT

KEEP NORFOLK P

W. FRED DUCKWORTH

N. B. ETHERIDGE

LAWRE

INK and VOTE

PROGRESSIVE

ROY B. MARTIN JR.

LINWOOD F. PERKINS

The June 6, 1958 Ledger-Dispatch and Star *ran a full-page paid political advertisement on behalf of W. Fred Duckworth's progressive team. The days of large councilmanic team advertisements such as this one have long passed.*

VOTE FOR THE
5-MAN TEAM

EQUESTING YOUR SUPPORT AS A FIVE-MAN TEAM realizing that as an individual no member can carry out any program—the team can. We have never, and will not now, make y wild, foolish and irresponsible promises. Anyone who would, is either totally ignorant and care-s of the city's financial responsibility or he thinks you are.

GUIDE BALLOT
GENERAL ELECTION
City of Norfolk
June 10, 1958

For Member of The City Council
(Vote For Five)

☒ W. F. DUCKWORTH *6301*

☒ L. C. PAGE *6264*

☒ N. B. ETHERIDGE *6349*

☒ ROY B. MARTIN, JR. *6660*

☒ LINWOOD F. PERKINS *6461*

☐ L. FRANCIS EVERETT *1641*

☐ FLOYD R. PLEDGER *2140*

☐ DREWRY LITTLE *1882*

 6

The councilmanic election of June 10, 1958, featured five incumbents pitted against three independents. The guide ballot shown here has Roy's notations of votes cast per candidate written next to each man's name. Roy, with 6,660 votes, was the front-runner in the election.

"Unquestionably, one of the most difficult periods that I was confronted with during my twenty-one years on Norfolk City Council was the closing of our schools. The commonwealth of Virginia had passed what was known as the Massive Resistance laws which in essence said that if any school was forced by federal courts to integrate, that school had to be closed." The legal basis for Virginia's law was grounded in John C. Calhoun's pre–Civil War doctrine of nullification, which meant, in simplest terms, that the states, based on the concept that each of the states had originally been sovereign and independent, could insert themselves between an unjust federal ruling or act of Congress if the federal action went against the best interest of states' rights as granted under the Constitution. States might, under Calhoun's theory, interpose their sovereignty to end the application of an unjust law. Virginia legislators spent a great deal of wrangling over interposition, thus amplifying the commonwealth's case to keep segregated public schools and bolstering the argument for Massive Resistance statewide. School integration as dictated by *Brown v. the Board of Education of Topeka, Kansas,* in 1954 was the ruling that sparked it all. The U.S. Supreme Court ruled that segregation of public education by race violated equal opportunity as guaranteed to every citizen of the country under the Fourteenth Amendment to the Constitution.

The integration issue, as far as Norfolk was concerned, was easing when in stepped Virginia Governor Thomas Bahnson Stanley (1954–58) with a threat to revoke funding for public school systems that integrated against the Massive Resistance orders in practice throughout the state. The federal courts, led by a ruling from one of their own, Judge Walter E. Hoffman of Norfolk, ruled that the schools must be opened and integrated under guidelines set forth by the federal government. The threat to revoke funding for the operation of public schools was very real and the implications far-reaching. If the State Supreme Court and a special three-judge panel sounded the death knell of the commonwealth's Massive Resistance laws, as both entities were expected to do, Virginia would have only a moral obligation to pay state funds for schools—not a legal one. In the event this happened, the only way the city of Norfolk would receive money needed to operate the schools would be by a bill passed at a special session of the General Assembly. The General Assembly was not inclined to look favorably to passage of such a bill if Norfolk became the first city in the state to integrate schools. It was also pointed out that by closing the remaining secondary schools, Norfolk would be running the risk of losing not only federal funds but also state funds for schools closed on the city's initiative. During the period Norfolk's public institutions were closed, a number of private schools were established to keep children in school until the situation could be rectified by further court rulings.

Through legal action, the city of Norfolk was required to integrate a number of its schools. "This was a terrible period in our city. It was one that brought the racial question more to the forefront. The council of the city of Norfolk took a position through an ordinance I thought made the situation more difficult. The mayor presented the council with an ordinance that closed schools beyond the sixth grade. He took the position that if part of the school system would be closed, then all the schools beyond the sixth grade should be closed also." Mayor Duckworth's proposal meant the closing of Booker T. Washington High School, already a secondary school for African Americans, all of the black junior high schools, and seventh grades in twenty-three white and ten black elementary schools. "I was quoted in the news media as having said, 'Gentlemen, we are today playing with the economic future of Norfolk.' When this came to a vote, I could not bring myself to vote to close more schools. My statement, which was well publicized at that time, indicated that I was not advocating integration, but that I just could not see the school system hurt anymore. The vote from council was 6 to 1." This vote to invoke a school fund cutoff plan was a harsh one, but it had some support in the Virginia General Assembly, which previously wrangled with the same issue. However, the dissenting vote, Martin's, was cast with sharp criticism of the state's role in helping localities with the school integration crisis. "This council," stated Martin to the media on January 13, 1959, "has assumed the leadership on the local level for the commonwealth of Virginia in support of the state's Massive Resistance laws. Norfolk has done so," he continued, "without the help or assistance the people of our city had hoped for and had every right to expect from Richmond." Martin pleaded that cutting off school funding was not the step that Governor Lindsay Almond's administration hoped would take place.

"I don't think that Mayor Duckworth, though we remained friends, ever got over the fact that I broke with the team on the school closure issue," recalled Martin. "I felt badly because I had always been a team player and wanted to be part of the progressive team that I thought we were at that time." Martin, absent satisfaction or conceited tone, remembered after casting his vote—and opinion—there were a number of people in the council chamber who applauded his actions. Citizens in attendance expected the usual 7 to 0 vote on school closure, and while his single vote did not change what happened—the schools closed—it was a decision that shocked both an expectant crowd and the man who cast it. Roy Martin readily admits that he was, indeed, stunned by the public's reaction. "I had not done this for integration, but I had done this for our schools."

"Through the years, I never received any real support from the black community," Martin recently said, "but I also admit that I never paid to get on the so-called Goldenrod ballot because I was opposed to what it stood for—currying favor in the African-American community with monetary contributions during elections." The Goldenrod ballot was in large measure the black community's response to a councilman's vote—if that councilman had joined their ballot—and the fact Martin was never supported by the black community was his refusal to join up. "This was something I felt I should not do and I certainly have not regretted it to this day." Opinion and fact on what the Goldenrod ballot entailed varies. Historically, it is no more than an important endorsement by key leaders in the black community of chosen candidates in an election, local, state, or federal. "Perhaps it initially served a purpose in bringing an awareness of the need to vote and participate in the political process among black citizens," said Martin in a *Ledger-Star* article on April 5, 1974. "But it reached the stage where a handful of people could direct a large bloc vote for certain candidates and ignore other candidates who had done much for the city." He remained a harsh critic of the Goldenrod's presence at polling places throughout Norfolk.

In response to his vote on school closure, Martin rebuked blacks in the audience for their response to his break with the city council, thus pushing a broader dividing line between himself and African Americans. "I don't appreciate the applause," he called that day above the din of clapping and the talk that seemed to consume everyone in the council chambers. Judge Joseph A. Jordan Jr., the first African American elected to the Norfolk City Council with his 1968 defeat of incumbent Paul Schweitzer and a longtime Martin opponent, remarked on Roy's retirement from council in 1974 that he was in the council chamber when the school closure vote was taken. "There were scores of people there," Jordan told a newspaper reporter years later, "many of them black. Martin got quite a reception from the audience, but instead of acknowledging us in a polite way, he rebuked those who responded." Jordan's point was broadly viewed as accurate of that day's events. Sam T. Barfield, former city councilman and retired commissioner of the revenue, remembered what "a very forceful man" Roy could be. "Sometimes he [was] so determined," Barfield continued, "that he offend[ed] his friends in his zeal to get things done. However, I don't know how he has been as patient as he is." But in many respects, Martin's view of the Goldenrod and its impact on elections was no harsher than his criticism of Sidney Kellam's lock on Virginia Beach politics that lasted for decades. By the time Roy retired from council in 1974, the Goldenrod had become, in effect, a political machine controlled by Jordan and his supporters.

The Virginia Supreme Court of Appeals and a special three-judge federal court panel were scheduled to hand down their ruling just a few days after the Norfolk City Council's 6 to 1 vote to close the schools. By acting in advance of the court's rulings, Norfolk's council was trying to dodge further litigation and, at least behind the scenes, state legislators and local politicians had done everything possible to keep Norfolk from being the first Virginia municipality to bow to integration of the schools. The fund cutoff simply bought the city time to allow the General Assembly to develop a totally new segregation plan for schools. Another factor, of course, and one not discussed a great deal was the city's desire to show the rest of the state how strongly city fathers felt about continuing segregated education. The commonwealth actually owed Norfolk $1.5 million for contractual expenses on closed white schools when the vote was taken, thus the council had no intention of jeopardizing the money obligated to city coffers.

"This is an illegal act and beyond the scope of your authority," stated Archie L. Boswell, attorney for the Norfolk Committee for Public Schools, after hearing the resolution to close the schools read before a packed council chambers. Boswell demanded further discussion, which did not occur. "Ten thousand children have been crying out for you to open the schools, and this will indicate that your answer is more closed schools. The state of Virginia," Boswell stated, "and Norfolk will have to hold their heads in shame . . . as my grandmother used to say, don't cut off your nose to spite your face." When the vote on the resolution was heard, Ocean

Black civic leader Mrs. W. T. Mason (right) asked city council not to be swayed by emotions in the Norfolk schools crisis. Mayor Duckworth is to the right of the American flag. (Neal V. Clark, photographer.)

View businessman C. H. Paul was compelled to address the city council: "Whenever you deny any child—white, black, red or yellow—from getting an education, you are hurting the whole country. God knows, I wish you hadn't done it." Paul went to say that there were not but seven states that have a sorrier education system than Virginia. "I'm a Virginian by adoption and proud of it—I'm a plain dumb North Carolinian—and just can't help voicing my objection. I'm sorry it happened and I hope none of you live to regret it." A *Virginian-Pilot* editorial published on January 14, 1959, stated that the "cruelest blow of all to the Norfolk public schools came not from the state's Massive Resistance program but from an action by the Norfolk City Council. The resolution passed by the Norfolk City Council," in the writer's view, "was an act of retaliation against Negro pupils [seventeen had registered at a white high school] that inflicts senseless punishment upon city schools." The editorial remarked further that the Massive Resistance laws of the state "are in the process of collapsing in the courts now," so Norfolk City Council could virtually count on school closings to be held in violation of the Fourteenth Amendment to the Constitution by the Fourth United States Court of Appeals. There was also good cause to believe that the State Supreme Court of Appeals would subsequently hold that the closing of the six Norfolk schools before the subsequent January 13 resolution, the Warren County High School, and two schools in Charlottesville, unconstitutional under Section 129 of the Virginia Constitution—for starters. The closure of Virginia schools violated not only several sections and subsections of the state constitution in Virginia, but also Norfolk's city charter.

If there was anything to be gained from this very difficult and unfortunate period in Norfolk's modern history, "it is that I believe the city of Norfolk overcame its most serious racial problems in the early stages of integration," said Martin. "We did not have the riots and demonstrations that were happening in many of America's larger cities. I have always felt that this matter was settled, not to the full satisfaction of either whites or blacks but in getting the schools open again. As the years have gone by, opening the schools again has been accepted as one of the reasons that we were able to keep the lid on what could have been a very explosive situation." In the end, however, there were more concrete ramifications to Virginia and Norfolk's closure of schools. Due to the Virginia General Assembly's move to withdraw financial support to its municipalities that would choose to integrate, Norfolk among them, and with the guidelines invoked by federal statute, the school system in Norfolk is today, as it has been since that time, in no way controlled by the city council other than appointing the school board and appropriating funds. As a result of Hoffman's rulings, the council has no control over how the school system of the city of Norfolk operates day to day.

The Norfolk City Council, shown here in a clipping from the January 29, 1959 Ledger-Dispatch, voted to reopen six of the city's integration-closed schools. Members of the council shown (left to right) are Roy B. Martin Jr., Linwood F. Perkins, Mayor W. Fred Duckworth, Lawrence C. Page, Lewis L. Layton, and (with his head barely visible, N. B. Etheridge. (Lawrence Maddry, photographer.)

Taken in Huntersville circa 1948, the living conditions for African-American and white families in sub-standard housing was deplorable, though one would never know it by the playful smiles on the faces of the children in the photograph. Residents used to say: "We were so poor, we didn't know we were poor." During W. Fred Duckworth's administration—and subsequently Roy Martin's—much of the slum housing in Norfolk was razed and replaced with public housing for lower-income tenants. (Author's collection.)

Mergers Gone Awry

Norfolk began a new decade much as it had the last—with substantial issues and projects spilling over on the weekly council docket—and the same mayor, W. Fred Duckworth. The year 1960 would be punctuated by high notes that while they have stood well apart from the turmoil of integration of schools that began six years earlier, thrust the emerging metropolis into a race to fine-tune and expand its boundaries and live up to the expectations of the seven-man team that lead city council. The task at hand would not be easy. Already the fledgling town of Virginia Beach and its surrounding neighbor, Princess Anne County, were pondering a merger.

As the winter wore on in Norfolk, the title of *All-America City* was added to recognition the city had earlier received for its fight against slum blight and degradation of the downtown area by the state. Norfolk was one of only eleven cities nationwide to be picked for the designation by the National Municipal League and *Look* magazine, which co-sponsored the contest for urban renewal initiatives that started in 1949. In choosing Norfolk for the award, the jury of prominent Americans making the pick cited the city for its three-phase program, begun a decade before, to combat inner-city blight. The jurors on the award panel, led by Dr. George H. Gallup, director of the American Institute of Public Opinion, also noted Norfolk's concerted and successful battle against organized vice and tuberculosis after the Second World War. Norfolk had cleared more than 326 acres of blighted housing and relocated some five thousand families. The jury also noted the city's new civic center, emerging medical center around Norfolk General Hospital, and Norfolk Industrial Park as major improvements to the Norfolk landscape. Only one other Southern city was conferred an All-America Award in 1960—Winston-Salem, North Carolina. Norfolk was the fourth Virginia community to be named to the All-America roster. Richmond won the award in 1950, Petersburg in 1953, and Roanoke in 1952. Norfolk had entered the competition with one hundred other cities. When it was chosen as a finalist in the fall of 1959, Colgate W. Darden Jr., former Virginia governor (1942–46), United States congressman (1933–37, 1939–41) and president of the University of Virginia (June 23, 1947–September 1, 1959), argued the city's case before the All-America City jury. After hearing the city won, Darden remarked that the program was "the most remarkable thing that has happened in Virginia," to a waiting pool of anxious reporters.

McIntosh Studio took this photograph at one of Norfolk Redevelopment and Housing Authority's public housing projects on September 13, 1954. (Courtesy of Kirn Library.)

As the city's projects heated up over the summer, Norfolk had a significant role in the marketing of $200 million in revenue bonds to finance a bridge-tunnel linking Hampton Roads with the Eastern Shore, one of the oldest and most important goals of Norfolk as a burgeoning port city. *The Richmond News Leader* went so far as to call the city's civic and business leaders who backed the project as "amazing men" who thought big and worked hard to get the desired results. A *Richmond Times-Dispatch* editorial of August 3, 1960, went further in its analysis of the bridge-tunnel initiative, quoting James S. Abrams of Allen and Company of New York City, one of the project's underwriters on the revenue bonds, as saying "Norfolk is on the threshold of an economic expansion on a par with what San Francisco faced in the mid-thirties when the Golden Gate reached the construction state." The *News Leader* editorial went on to say of Norfolk's community leaders: "Their program of slum clearance, urban renewal, street construction, and general public improvements looks to an exciting future. To visit Norfolk these days," the editorial continued, "is to visit a city humming with activity. Some three years hence, when the bridge-tunnel opens, that activity will increase as the worst obstacle to coastal truck and passenger traffic is removed." The anticipated completion date of the seventeen-mile bridge-tunnel, January of 1964, was late by only four months, opening on April 15 to traffic.

The city council elections in June 1960 saw two significant changes to the seven-man ticket long held together by Mayor Duckworth. Sam T. Barfield defeated Lawrence C. Page, one of the mayor's ardent supporters, but the weakest of the incumbents seeking reelection. While the two maintained a cordial relationship, Barfield was not a Duckworth booster on council. Paul Schweitzer was elected to his first four-year term. Barfield's presence did not prevent Duckworth from being elected to an unprecedented sixth two-year term as president of the city council, a title that carried with it the honorary title of mayor, on September 1, despite Barfield's vote against him. The 5 to 1 vote for mayor had not been seen since Duckworth was first elected mayor by his peers in 1950. Vice Mayor N. B. Etheridge was returned to his position on council by unanimous vote. When called to vote first by temporary chairman Roy Martin, Barfield read a statement which said, in effect, that while he thought the mayor deserved the thanks of each and every one of Norfolk's citizens for his service, it was time for him to step aside. "As I continually stated during my campaign," read Barfield, "I oppose the process of self-perpetuation of council and the practice of the mayor succeeding himself for more than two terms."

The acerbity of the relationship between Barfield, the mayor, and Roy Martin would continue for the duration of Barfield's tenure on city council. Two months after beginning his council term, Barfield was told at a November 1 council meeting to "either keep his campaign pledge and stay away from city council's 'informal' meetings or stop complaining about them," which Luther J. Carter, *The Virginian-Pilot* staff writer, noted was a message spoken by Martin on behalf of himself, Mayor W. Fred Duckworth, and four other Duckworth administration colleagues. Roy's comment was described as "a bristling statement" in reply to one by Barfield a day earlier. Barfield had run for city council on an antiadministration platform, one opposed to the council's closed-door meetings. While opposed to the sessions,

Barfield had been attending them to accommodate City Manager Thomas F. Maxwell, but that he was not coming away from the meetings being fully aware of what was going on in the city of Norfolk. His motion to abolish the closed-door sessions was quashed on September 13. Martin was not willing to let Barfield's statement go unchallenged. The full text of his remarks was read into the council record. The crux of his pointed admonition of Barfield noted, among other pertinent corrections to Barfield's statements, that the council was "not aware of Mr. Barfield leaving any meeting held in Mr. Maxwell's office before the balance of the council. If he has been doing as he says, it certainly has not been obvious to the other members of this body. To my knowledge, Mr. Barfield has attended every Monday morning meeting that I have attended and has left with the rest of the group when we depart at the end of the morning's discussions." While the banter between Barfield and the rest of council was far from over, issues of broader importance for Norfolk and the region had begun stirring in the spring of 1960. Suddenly, by the fall of that year, personal squabbles on council were let go and the seven-man team was just that—a team—again. The issue that bound them together—annexation—would have far-reaching ramifications for the old port city as none before or since.

"The proposed merger of Princess Anne County and the small town of Virginia Beach is probably one of the most historically damaging moves that has ever been incurred by the city of Norfolk," Roy Martin has remarked in recent months. "After the annexation of Princess Anne County, Sidney S. Kellam, a community leader in Princess Anne County and very influential in state politics, came to the Norfolk City Council and asked that we make an agreement regarding annexation." In April of 1960, Kellam asked Norfolk to agree to wait a period of five years before proceeding with any additional annexation in Princess Anne County and, in return, the county would agree not to ask the Virginia General Assembly to change any of the state's extant annexation laws. Knowing the cost of taking care of the recently annexed area, the city council was very receptive to such a proposal and immediately accepted it.

"Unfortunately, in 1961, Sidney Kellam proposed the merger of Princess Anne County and the town of Virginia Beach, which came as a complete shock to all of us at the Norfolk City Council," noted Martin. The reaction to Kellam's proposal was not well received by Norfolk. Norfolk attempted several maneuvers to bring Kellam's merger proposal to a screeching halt, including an advertisement depicting what the city thought about the merger and how it would affect the people involved. Sidney Kellam made the statement at the time his plan was announced that he anticipated the town and county's merger to precipitate a larger scale metropolitan government for the Hampton Roads area. He added the merger, as he proposed it, at least practiced what he preached on regional governance, hinting his peers in Norfolk could take a cue and do more practicing than preaching. The relationship between Kellam and his counterparts in Norfolk cooled considerably after his proposal was made public.

"I always felt Norfolk had the potential for being one of the greatest cities in America if we could continue along the path of steady geographical growth," regretted Martin. "When the proposed merger of Princess Anne and Virginia Beach came about, I felt all the more that the merger of those two should include Norfolk." Martin made a proposal of his own at the council meeting in early November 1961, much to the surprise of his colleagues, that the city provide its proportionate share of the cost to start investigating the feasibility of a three-way merger with the town of Virginia Beach, Princess Anne, including the initiation of meetings with the people of all three of these areas in 1962. The council voted unanimously to authorize Mayor Duckworth to arrange a meeting between the governing bodies of the two cities and the county.

In late October 1962, the city of Norfolk used a four-page newspaper advertisement to inform Princess Anne County residents that the county's imminent merger with Virginia Beach was a mistake that would threaten the progressive vitality of the Hampton Roads area. Virginia Beach and Princess Anne County officials charged that Norfolk was interfering in matters that were none of its business, and in subsequent communications with their representatives, the Norfolk City Council soon learned the ad served more to solidify support for the merger between the county and Virginia Beach than deter it.

In a follow-up editorial, Kellam's reaction to Martin's proposal was pointed, both barrels leveled to fire on Roy, Mayor Duckworth and the Norfolk City Council. "If Norfolk is going to dictate the pattern of growth in the area, then there is no use meeting on a possible three-way merger. But if it's for the benefit of all our citizens, I am confident that the governing bodies could sit down and talk." A few days later, on November 10, *The Virginian-Pilot* editorial page remarked that "Mr. Martin has caught the city by surprise. He seems to clearly have caught Princess Anne County and Virginia Beach by surprise. If it seems likely, he also has caught his own colleagues by surprise. It is easier to understand the unusual reaction on the council advertisements of October 28th and 29th and its unanimous agreement now with the Martin proposal." But the editorial went further to say: "So the Martin proposal is an altogether fresh and imaginative approach, strikingly different in spirit and in content from the ideas and attitude of the council's formal statement in its advertisement. Mr. Martin is taking a harder and a deeper look. He has come up with something that deserves and we hope will receive, serious examination."

The Pilot editorial may have held out more optimism than should or could have been expected from the political behind-the-scenes machinations by Sidney Kellam and Charles B. Cross, his South Norfolk peer, to create the independent cities of Virginia Beach and Chesapeake, respectively. Despite the fact the mergers were a "done deal" in the General Assembly, a proposed three-way merger meeting came about at a luncheon held by the city of Norfolk at the Pinetree Inn in Princess Anne County. At the end of that meeting, Sidney Kellam and Mayor Duckworth met jointly for a press conference. It was at that time that Kellam took the position that

Council Votes Cutoff
Of Va. Beach's Water

Mayor Attacks Merger

By RAYMOND L. BANCROFT

Virginian-Pilot Staff Writer

NORFOLK — The water-cutoff threat became ominous Tuesday when Norfolk City Council voted 5 to 1 to end its water service to Virginia Beach Dec. 31, 1962, if the proposed Beach-Princess Anne merger succeeds.

Councilman Paul Schweitzer voted against the cutoff, which is contingent upon the city attorney's ruling that it would be legal. Vice Mayor N. B. Etheridge did not attend the meeting.

Councilman Roy B. Martin Jr. meanwhile proposed a meeting of the governing bodies of Norfolk, South Norfolk and Norfolk County to discuss the possibility of a three-way consolidation study.

Council voted unanimously to have City Manager Thomas F. Maxwell arrange the meeting and on Mayor W. Fred Duckworth's suggestion, also invited Portsmouth City Council to attend. Prompting Martin's suggestion were the talks begun Monday night between Norfolk County and South Norfolk on a possible merger into a new city.

DUCKWORTH ACTION

Mayor Duckworth proposed the water cutoff.

He said he understood the city's contract with Virginia Beach to supply water at bulk rates will expire Dec. 31, 1962.

The proposed merger would become fact the next day — Jan. 1, 1963. It has been approved by the Virginia Beach and Princess Anne governing bodies, and will be decided on in a referendum next month.

Under terms of the three-year water contract, either party can end it on six months' written notice.

"We're being charitable in that we're giving them 13 months notice," Duckworth said.

Schweitzer, who is chairman of the board of Layne-Atlantic Co., a water supply contracting firm, said:

"I think any engineer will say it is impossible to set up a new water-supply system in that time. You can't shut the water off on thousands of persons. You're stating here a specific shutoff date.

"I think we should go into negotiations on a specific time with Virginia Beach," Schweitzer added.

Duckworth, in a prepared statement on the water situation, said:

"I do not know what this or future councils of the city of Norfolk may do about the city of Norfolk furnishing water for another city.

"I would think that they would take a long, hard look at proposals to increase our present in-

(See Council, Page 9)

Mayor Duckworth's resolution to cutoff water to Virginia Beach drew this headline in The Virginian-Pilot *on December 6, 1961. The motion passed 5 to 1, but soon had three city councilmen pleading they had misunderstood the language of the resolution.*

he would be happy to talk merger with Norfolk when all parties could sit down as equals. In fewer words than Kellam used that day, he wanted a piece of the Norfolk power pie, but it was not proffered by Duckworth. The press conference, in essence, gave every indication that the meeting had been a formality. Kellam and his constituency had no intention of going ahead with such a three-way merger unless county and Virginia Beach residents demanded it. The merger question went before the people of Princess Anne County and Virginia Beach and they over-whelmingly voted for the two-way merger that was already set to take place on January 1, 1963.

When Virginia Beach and Princess Anne County voted to merge, Mayor Duckworth presented an ordinance to the Norfolk City Council which stated when the present water contract with Princess Anne County and Norfolk city expired, Norfolk would no longer issue permits for new waterlines into Virginia Beach. Duckworth's proposed ordinance, unfortunately "misunderstood" by mem-bers of the council, was passed by a margin of 5 to 1 on December 5, 1961. Only after further review and discussion by three of the council members—Martin, Linwood Perkins, and Sam Barfield—was the proposal defeated. "I in no sense voted to cut off water," Martin said the following day. "I thought we were looking for information to determine whether we could or not." Barfield claimed the same. Mayor Duckworth's official motion as recorded in the minutes of the council stat-ed as follows:

> *I move that we request the city manager and city attorney to investigate the water matter and if my findings are correct, that they notify the city of Virginia Beach that we will discontinue the water supply as of December 31, 1962, provided they (Virginia Beach and Princess Anne County) become a city.*

Councilman Lewis L. Layton appeared to have understood the motion per-fectly. "My understanding was that the mayor was requesting that if he was correct in his findings, that Virginia Beach be notified of the termination of the water con-tract." Duckworth's only comment on hearing about the confusion was terse: "That was the motion and they voted for it." He later told a *Virginian-Pilot* reporter that the council was being "charitable in that we're giving them thirteen months notice" of the cutoff. As the council became embroiled in the interpreta-tion of the original motion, two versions of the motion emerged—one the mayor filed with the city clerk and the other a close, but dissimilar, reading of the motion obtained by Barfield, also from the city clerk's office. Duckworth's version a couple of days after the original reading added "the expiration of the contract," after the date December 31, 1962, the day before, it should be duly noted, the merger would be final and the city of Virginia Beach officially recognized in the com-monwealth. Barfield's version was the one recorded in council minutes—and his own hand—that day. *The Virginian-Pilot* editorial page confirmed Barfield's inter-pretation in its December 7 editorial on the matter. Clearly, said *The Pilot*, "This is different language from the motion which Councilman Barfield said yesterday he obtained early in the day from the city clerk. It is different in intent, purpose, and scope from the intent and purpose which Councilmen Martin and Perkins said yesterday they had in mind when they voted." Better yet, interjected *The Pilot* editorialist, the Norfolk City Council should have been asking itself "how this confusion originated, why two versions of the Duckworth motion are in circulation, and whether other pertinent details and circumstances need explanation."

Mayor Duckworth issued a formal statement for the record that made clear his view of furnishing water to another city. In his bristling barrage aimed squarely at Sidney Kellam, Duckworth said: "I would think that [future city councils] would take a long, hard look at proposals to increase our present investment in our water system to encourage the development of a city which has been formed for the explicit purpose of preventing the expansion of the city of Norfolk." Perhaps his view was drawn from years of experience dealing with the Princess Anne County political machine, but Duckworth's concluding paragraph was a parting shot at his old foes to the east like no other:

> *If the city is shut off from any possibility of expansion by the proposed consolidation of Virginia Beach and Princess Anne County, I would think that any city council charged with the protection of the city's interests would decide that it was not in the interest of the city to worry about the water supply of a competing rather than a cooperating area outside the city.* (The Virginian-Pilot, December 6, 1961.)

The implications of the original ordinance would have spelled a huge mistake for the future economic development of the region, not to mention the black eye it would have given Norfolk with Virginia Beach residents. If Norfolk had towed the line on the ordinance and refused new water lines into the new city, Virginia Beach would not have grown to the extent it has today. The arrangement with Princess Anne County also differed from the deal Norfolk had cut with the town of Virginia Beach in the nineteen twenties. Princess Anne County did not have a water system of its own and relied solely on Norfolk, which billed water to county residents and businesses at double the city rate. Virginia Beach, by virtue of its pre-existing contracts with the city of Norfolk, had its own water distribution system within its corporate limits and in the parts of Princess Anne County to the town's north. Virginia Beach sold its water to customers, despite the ownership of its own distribution system, at a little over twice the price-per-thousand-gallon rate it paid Norfolk for the water, so there was no advantage to the town's residents.

A couple of days after the initial vote on the water cutoff, a four-man majority consisting of Martin, Barfield, Perkins, and Paul Schweitzer publicly stated their interest in killing the original council vote on Duckworth's motion. Despite its landlocked status, "particularly when you reflect today on what the Virginia Beach and Princess Anne County merger action meant to Norfolk," Martin recalled, "you realize that this city, through its own efforts, has continued to prosper while not growing in land area and not growing in population, but certainly growing in importance as the business, financial, educational, and cultural center of Hampton Roads." Of course, the Virginia Beach–Princess Anne County merger was not the only merger gone awry, so it is perhaps doubly remarkable that Norfolk has achieved its present success.

Norfolk County officials had watched with great interest the unfolding drama between the city of Norfolk and the proposed merger of Princess Anne County and the town of Virginia Beach. Colon L. Hall, then chairman of the Norfolk County Board of Supervisors, told a reporter with *The Virginian-Pilot* that he felt strongly his county should complete its merger discussions with South Norfolk before entertaining talks with the city of Norfolk. At the same session of the General Assembly that allowed the merger of Virginia Beach and Princess Anne County, a delegation from Norfolk County and the city of South Norfolk requested a bill asking that they be allowed to merge following the same route that Virginia Beach and Princess Anne County had taken. When they were allowed to merge, the city of Chesapeake was born, like her new neighbor Virginia Beach, in 1963. After the General Assembly agreed to these two mergers, it completely locked in Norfolk and Portsmouth, thereby ending any and all opportunity for the two cities to expand their corporate boundaries. The mergers which occurred in the 1962–63 time frame exposed the unique—and often detrimental—impact of Virginia not having cooperative growth mechanisms in place between county and city governments in the commonwealth. Although Norfolk's population was over 300,000 when Virginia Beach and Chesapeake city formations occurred, it has dropped off to around quarter of a million today while the population of Virginia Beach (and what was then Princess Anne County) skyrocketed from about 100,000 in 1963 to over 450,000 at present. There are over 100,000 people a day commuting to work in Norfolk.

Norfolk Asks to Join Merger

Roy Martin

(Continued from Page 1)

to add: "I don't mean to ~~st~~ it is a delaying action."

~~was~~ Kellam who appeared at ~~Nor~~folk City Council meeting in ~~~~ 1960 and suggested ~~~~" to a ~~battle~~ ~~~~ation.

'Monkey Where It Belongs'

P.A. Nudged on Water

~~~~ years ~~~~ed not to try ~~~~ state annexation laws ~~~~ General Assembly for a ~~~~eriod.

~~Nor~~folk also agreed ~~~~icy of extending ~~~~e county to ser~~~~ ~~~~evelopments. T~~~~ ~~~~its water servic~~ ~~~~ to prevent the ~~~~ing for ann~~~~ ~~~~es.

They'll Set

~~ING~~ DONE

~~~~am also propo~~~~ ~~~~eeting that Tid~~~~ ~~~~es set up a committee to ~~~~ the Metropolitan form of ~~~~ment. The committee met ~~~~ times but nothing has ~~~~done since.

Water Talk

~~~~ope the pattern we are try~~~~ ~~~~ set in Princess Anne and ~~~~ia Beach will lead to an ~~~~ Metro government for the ~~~~ater area," Kellam said ~~~~sday.

With City

~~~~re practicing what we're ~~~~ing," he added.

~~~~in referred to the Metro ~~~~ his statement.

"To the disappointment of many who had great hopes of the success of this Metro plan. ~~~~ find nothing has ~~~~ plished un ~~~~ ~~~~said.

SCHWEITZER DUBIOUS

Only Councilman Paul Schweitzer doubts about Martin's proposal.

~~~~st I've heard ~~~~aid. "This is ~~~~ going into." ~~~~st the Metro ~~~~d him. ~~~~all," Schweit~~~~

~~~~u exclude the ~~~~ in the Metro ~~~~ South Norfolk ~~~~y) from your ~~~~proposal? Schweitzer asked Martin.

"Wouldn't it be more logic~~~~ and feasible to have a three-w~~~~ merger now?" Martin asked ~~~~answer. "This is the time ~~~~any merger is to be bro~~~~ about.

'THE THIRD PART'

"Why don't we copy what Hampton, Newport News and Warwick attempted and see what we can do?" he continued. "If these people are sincere, I'd like

to see Norfolk become the third part of this merger proposal."

Several years ago, the cities ~~~~ Newport News, Warwick and ~~Ham~~pton tried to consolidate into ~~a~~ massive Peninsula city. Vot~~~~ ~~~~ Newport News and War~~~~ ~~~~ approved the plan but Hampton residents voted against it. Then in 1958 Warwick and Newport News consolidated.

But Martin said other communities interested in the Metro plan for this area are welcome to join in the proposal.

"The more the better," he said. "I want Norfolk to get in on any Metro plan, and if South Norfolk, Norfolk County and Portsmouth want to come in, it's all right."

'MAKES GOOD SENSE'

Mayor Duckworth said Martin's plan "makes good sense."

"I can certainly see if this plan is put forward that it would ~~Pr~~incess Anne taxpayers a ~~~~t of money," ~~~~

for us at t~~~~ a lack of it at others. ~~~~ like them to be consistent."

Other city councilmen generally approved Martin's plan.

"I'm in favor of the study and

might be against the plan," Mayor N. B. Etheridge sa~~id~~

"If Kellam is sincere wit~~h~~ Metro plan, he can't den~~~~ chance for us to sit down an~~~~ cuss it," Councilman Sam T.~~~~ field said.

'BEDROOM COMMUNITY'

"I think it's an excellent ~~~~gestion," Councilman L. L. ~~~~ton said. "Until the whole ~~~~is built up, Princess Anne ~~~~ to be Norfolk's bed~~~~

Norfolk Requests To Join Merger

~~~~way merge~~~~ ~~~~held, it must be done ~~~~ly ~~~~ county board and Virginia ~~~~ City Council are expected t~~~~

★　★　★　★　★　★　★　★

Roy Martin's vision for a "great new Tidewater city" carried over into the prominent article in The Virginian-Pilot *of November 9, 1961, and many to follow, including "P.A. Nudged on Water," by* Pilot *political reporter Raymond L. Bancroft on May 30, 1962.*

Perhaps the most enduring photograph of General of the Army Douglas A. MacArthur is this one, taken as he waded ashore at Leyte, Philippine Islands, in October 1944 during the landings to retake the islands from the Japanese. (Official United States Army photograph.)

The Old Soldier Bids Farewell

Shortly after General of the Army Douglas A. MacArthur returned to the United States from the front lines of the conflict in Korea after his well-publicized dismissal by President Harry S. Truman in April of 1951, he was invited to Norfolk for the dedication of a park in honor of his mother, the former Mary Pinckney Hardy, who was born in the city's Berkley section. The business leadership of Norfolk had acquired the old Hardy home, *Riveredge*, the home of his mother's family, and taken brick from it to use as the foundation for a wall around a small, but attractive, park at the foot of what was then the old Berkley Bridge. The general and his wife, Jean, and their son, Arthur, readily agreed to come to the city for the dedication of the park in Mary Hardy MacArthur's honor. "Little did I realize," Martin would say later, "as I stood on the corner of Sewell's Point Road [now Little Creek Road] and Granby Street with my one-year-old son on my shoulders and watched the MacArthur family's arrival at the airport, how closely related I would be linked in the years to come to the MacArthur story." (Yes, Norfolk Airport was then near Wards Corner.) The MacArthur story to which Roy so warmly refers became a poignant chapter in Norfolk history that would conclude solemnly on a frigid day in January 2000 with the interment of the general's wife, Jean, next to her general in the rotunda of the MacArthur Memorial.

"Mayor Duckworth and I were going to a municipal meeting in New York on November 27, 1960, when he advised me that he had contacted MacArthur's staff to arrange an appointment for the two of us to meet the general. Our objective was to assess the general's plans to disperse his memorabilia and papers," which were later adjudged to be extensive. The meeting was held at the general's penthouse in The Waldorf-Astoria, located on New York's posh Park Avenue. "I was tremendously impressed with the general. He couldn't have been warmer and treated Mayor Duckworth as though they had been friends for years. He was equally as cordial with me." Roy would say at the time that MacArthur's penthouse "was the most beautiful I had ever seen." More recently, he recalled that after the initial pleasantries, "Mayor Duckworth came right to the point, as was his custom, and told the general that we would like to know his plans for selection of a repository for his paper archive and impressive memorabilia." The general advised Duckworth and Martin that there

Major General Courtney Whitney (left), MacArthur's aide, discusses an agreement with Norfolk officials for the MacArthur Memorial at a conference held in City Hall on February 2, 1961. With Whitney in the Neal V. Clark photograph, which ran in the next day's Virginian-Pilot, *are Norfolk Mayor W. Fred Duckworth and Councilman Roy B. Martin Jr.*

were a number of places that were anxious to get the items, inclusive of the U.S. Military Academy at West Point, the Smithsonian Institution, and a respectable roster of public and private universities. It was serendipitous that Mayor Duckworth had asked for and secured the appointment when he did because Jean MacArthur was growing increasingly concerned that her husband make some provisions for his material. Responding to MacArthur's initial reply, Duckworth, again, came to the point. "He said to MacArthur: 'If you place that material in those places you've named, it would be lost. If you were to put it in the city of Norfolk, it would be one of the finest things that this community has.' I think this statement sold the general immediately, for he gave every consideration in putting the memorabilia in Norfolk."

MacArthur already had a favorable impression of Norfolk. When he came on his last visit to the city on November 18, 1951, some four months before his famous "Old soldiers never die" speech before a joint session of Congress, the general came to Norfolk to officially dedicate the memorial in the city's Berkley section to his mother. Mayor Duckworth, who had met MacArthur and his family at the airport and rode with him to services at St. Paul's Episcopal Church and then to the dedication ceremony, remembered later that the general gleaned his first positive image of the city at that time. "In fact," remarked Duckworth, "the city council created a special category of honorary citizen and General MacArthur was presented with certificate number one." Afterward, the city, largely through Duckworth, remained in contact with MacArthur through letters and personal visits.

Before Duckworth and Martin left the general's suite that day in November 1960, arrangements were made for them to meet MacArthur's personal assistant, Major General Courtney Whitney, later that evening. At the conclusion of the meeting, arrangements were made to bring Whitney to Norfolk in mid-December to view the city's possible accommodations for MacArthur's papers and memorabilia. The visit took place shortly thereafter. Roy escorted Whitney around Norfolk, showing him various areas being considered for MacArthur's collection. One of the first plans offered by the city, though it was eventually scrapped, had been to build a freestanding structure at the Norfolk Division of the College of William and Mary (now Old Dominion University). But, in the meantime, a better opportunity—and solution—presented itself. The city had a new civic center complex under construction to consolidate public offices and courts. The new center would replace, among other public buildings scattered throughout downtown, the old courthouse, which had been the original City Hall. The old City Hall seemed the perfect site for MacArthur's archive. Since this was also a historic building and not slated for demolition in the city's urban renewal plan, an alternative use needed to be found for the structure, which was also much in need of repairs. "When I showed this building to General Whitney, he agreed wholeheartedly that it was beautiful and it had every possibility of becoming a wonderful museum. At this point in time, there was no indication the building would be anything more than a repository for the memorabilia and papers." However, soon after Whitney's return to New York, Mayor Duckworth received a message from him—a request from the MacArthurs that caught the mayor a bit off guard. General MacArthur and his wife wanted to know if they could be buried in the museum as well. Having no conventional home, Douglas MacArthur chose a spiritual one. The scope of the project then grew from a museum to memorial. MacArthur requested his burial in Norfolk rather than his plot in Arlington National Cemetery because he felt Washington, D.C., had become emblematic of his one great personal defeat—his firing by Truman—and, therefore, he would prefer to be interred in the birthplace of his mother.

General MacArthur presented Mayor Duckworth with stipulations on the building that was to be his memorial. He did not want the city council to solicit any donations for the building as many proposals of that kind had been presented to him in the past and he had firmly declined. MacArthur, through General Whitney, also communicated to the mayor that should the city opt to take his material, and should the general decide to give it to Norfolk, it must be put in a location where it could be seen by the public with no admission charge. "It was also understood," Mayor Duckworth would recall later, "that it would be open to the public at large with no restrictions as to race or creed." General MacArthur's third stipulation was a request that if the agreement was entered into by the city of

Norfolk, that a Japanese garden be erected either around or on the side of the building because of his high regard for the Japanese people. With the majority of his conditions guaranteed by the Norfolk City Council, MacArthur was satisfied.

MacArthur's unconditional approval of Norfolk as the repository for his collection was immediately forthcoming on December 26, with details to follow. "As a Virginian myself," said the general, "whose mother came from a long line of Virginians, and whose mother and father were married in the present city of Norfolk, I accept as a great honor the invitation of the city to place my papers, decorations and other mementos of my military service in its perpetual care and keeping." On February 2, 1961, Major General Courtney Whitney, on a scheduled visit to the city, accepted a proposed deed of trust for a museum to house the memorabilia of General MacArthur. The proposed deed of trust was drawn by Judge William L. Parker, special attorney to the project and president of the board of trustees of the Norfolk Museum of Arts and Sciences, in consultation with the city attorney, Leonard H. Davis.

The proposed MacArthur Memorial did not escape the veil of controversy that enveloped many post–World War II projects in the city. Councilman Roy Martin recommended a public hearing on the MacArthur Memorial at the city council meeting of March 27, 1961, to smooth the groundswell of opposition brewing over the city's offer to the general. While the controversy, if it could be called such, was minimal compared to projects both before and after it, attorney James A. Howard was determined to give the opposition a voice on the editorial pages of the Norfolk newspapers. "I realize that we're not obligated to hold a public hearing on the memorial," said Martin at the time, "but in order to take any stigma away from the memorial and to show that the reasonable people of Norfolk are behind it, I ask that the council give consideration to having a public hearing as soon as possible." The council approved the hearing. Howard, in council chambers for the vote, spoke for the opposition when he noted that he and those he represented did not object to the memorial, but to the way the city council had chosen to spend taxpayer dollars without making known the council's plans until the project was a "done" deal. "There is opposition to the memorial," said Howard as he took the speaker's podium at the council meeting. "The only opposition I've heard I can count on the fingers of one hand," retorted Martin. "Where is this opposition?" inquired Mayor Duckworth. "It's been in the newspapers," replied Howard firmly. "The newspapers?" queried the mayor. "Yes, in the letters to the editor column," replied Howard. "Oh," said Duckworth, "I don't read letters to the editor."[4] While the exchange between Duckworth, Martin, and Howard remained cordial, Howard was determined to stay at the heels of the council until satisfied that the cost of the project was a reasonable one. He was against what he called "a blank check" policy where the memorial to MacArthur was concerned and he was not alone. Howard, in the end, did not prevail at the subsequent public hearing on the memorial—and this is fortunate. In the long term, Frank Batten, then president of the Chamber of Commerce, said the chamber's convention bureau believed the MacArthur Memorial to be a tremendous attraction for the city aside from it being a place of honor for the nation's greatest soldier.

The most unfortunate outcome of the memorial controversy, however, was the rancor which developed between a group called Protectors of the Public Fund, an organization vehemently opposed to the Democratic political machine that ran city government at that time. The group's spokesperson, Constance Freeman Griffin, attended nearly every city council meeting in which a vote was to be taken on allocation of public money for the MacArthur Memorial—and the Moses Myers House. The Myers property, circa 1792, was being restored by the Norfolk Museum of Arts and Sciences and required city funds to complete the plans as they had been presented and approved by the council. The exchanges between Griffin and Martin, in particular, grew abusive on both sides. When Martin accused Griffin of being paid by an antiadministration group to berate the council on its MacArthur Memorial spending, Griffin denied it, snapping back: "I am not being paid. I am acting just as a citizen interested in the best interests of the city."[5] Griffin, often described in the newspapers as "a thorn in the council's side," was not willing to back down. More than a concerned citizen, Griffin was the granddaughter of former Norfolk city councilman and architect Joel Callis White, and grew up used to the bantering between council and citizens on matters in which public money had been allocated. While the city moved forward with final plans and specifications on the memorial, Griffin pressed her point with council at nearly every session from March 21 well into the summer months. Perhaps misunderstood by council, perhaps not, she once said that it was more important to her that everyone know the group she formed was not against the memorial, just "the use of public funds for it." There was no room for Constance Griffins during Mayor Duckworth's administration. Accustomed to having his way, Duckworth and his allies on council, including Martin, quickly squelched dissention and moved on, more often in their desire to see good projects come to fruition than to cap productive public debate. Norfolk, in many respects, sat teetering on the brink of success or failure during the Duckworth administration. All that would come to pass over the decades that followed rested squarely on the shoulders of a mayor who carried the values of another generation into a time of complex issues and change in which race and creed altered the social landscape, and public debate was the norm, not an anomaly. The fact Duckworth, and to a large extent, Roy, did not enjoy public debate originated with what drove them to public service in the first place— a vision for what could be. The MacArthur Memorial debate exposed public dissention on a major project in such a way that neither the mayor or city councilmen could have been expected to demonstrate great patience, and that they largely held their tongues when berated weekly was probably a minor miracle. However, the council's exchanges on the memorial and subsequent projects raised the specter that the Duckworth team ought to listen to what the newspapers dubbed the "silent voices" that did not come to council chambers, but whose views lived vicariously in the cautionary word of Mrs. Griffin. The MacArthur Memorial project proceeded with an estimated price tag of $525,000—worthy of every penny spent—to convert the old City Hall for the general's museum and crypt. Though the cost would eventually exceed the amount stated in 1961, the city emerged with a jewel in Norfolk's crown like no other.

General Douglas MacArthur (center) enters Walter Reed Army Hospital in Washington, D.C., on March 2, 1964. Left to right: Jean MacArthur, the general's wife since 1936; Major General A. L. Tynes; General MacArthur; and Lieutenant General Leonard D. Heaton, U.S. Army Surgeon-General. MacArthur died of liver and kidney failure after undergoing three major surgeries in seventeen days on April 5. (Photograph by Mr. Hohman of the Post Photographic Facility at Fort Holabird, Maryland.)

Attorney General of the United States Robert F. Kennedy and his wife, Ethel, leave St. Paul's Episcopal Church after solemn rites for General MacArthur concluded on April 11, 1964. The Kennedys are accompanied from the church by Admiral and Mrs. H. P. Smith and behind the admiral, Virginia Governor Albertis Harrison. The original photograph was taken by William Abourjille, a Ledger-Star *photographer, and ran in the evening paper's edition that day.*

On Friday, June 1, 1962, the mayor met with Major General Whitney in Norfolk and made several detailed proposals to be taken to MacArthur in New York. With the general's permission, the city wanted to create a national, nonprofit, tax-exempt corporation to be known as the Douglas MacArthur Foundation or the Douglas MacArthur Fund, to hold and administer gifts made to it for educational, scientific, and charitable purposes. The corporation was to have three trustees at its inception, with provision for a maximum of seven. Any additional trustees beyond the original three were to be elected by the original trustees. The impetus behind the foundation was to provide scholarships to college-level students—without restriction to race and creed—based on their study of American history. The foundation would also be the repository of monies used to enlarge and maintain items in the museum.

The old City Hall building, its 1850 Classic Revival architectural style commanding the street, required extensive refurbishment to accommodate MacArthur's museum and crypt. Architects William and Geoffrey Platt of New York City were retained to design the new interior of the memorial. Geoffrey Platt had been recently appointed chief advisor on the preservation of historic buildings

Norfolk officials attended MacArthur's funeral en masse, including (in civilian attire) former Norfolk Mayor W. Fred Duckworth (foreground left) and City Councilman Linwood F. Perkins (right). Behind Duckworth was Second District Congressman Porter Hardy Jr. and following Hardy, then Norfolk Mayor Roy Martin. (William Abourjille, photographer.)

in New York City by Mayor Robert Ferdinand Wagner Jr. (1954–65). Norfolk architect Finlay F. Ferguson Jr. acted as the architectural coordinator for the memorial's refurbishment, and the contractor hired was E. T. Gresham.

Newly elected Mayor Roy Martin visited General MacArthur in his New York City penthouse in late December 1963 to discuss plans for the memorial's opening the following January. Accompanied by City Manager Thomas F. Maxwell, former Mayor Duckworth, then head of the MacArthur Memorial Foundation, and Samuel T. Northern, director of the city's new community promotion office, Martin and his party presented MacArthur with photographs of the museum interior, which he called "magnificent," and talked at length about the type of ceremony the general preferred during the building's opening and dedication events.

The opening ceremony for the General Douglas MacArthur Memorial was held on Sunday, January 26, 1964, General MacArthur's eighty-fourth birthday. He was scheduled to be in Norfolk on May 30 for the formal dedication of the building, but he died at Walter Reed Army Hospital in Washington, D.C., on April 5 of liver and kidney failure. "With the death of General Douglas MacArthur we witness the passing of one of the most brilliant and colorful military leaders of modern times," read then Mayor Roy Martin from a prepared statement published

Norfolk's former City Hall building was converted to a museum and final resting place for General of the Army Douglas A. MacArthur and his wife, Jean, in between 1961 and 1964. Staff Sergeant Louis Castagnaro shot this photograph, taken on March 31, 1964, a few weeks after the general's interment. (Official United States Army photograph.)

An interior view of the rotunda of the MacArthur Memorial showing the crypt area was shot by Staff Sergeant Louis Castagnaro on March 31, 1964. (Official United States Army photograph.)

Norfolk bade a quiet farewell to Jean MacArthur, who died on Saturday, January 22, 2000, at the age of 101. While tens of thousands of onlookers attended the funeral of the general in 1964, only two people stood by silently as Jean MacArthur's casket was carried up the steps of the memorial for internment beside her husband. The ceremony of January 27 was private, attended by dignitaries, old friends, and her son. There was a wreath-laying the following day attended by (left to right) Norfolk Mayor Paul D. Fraim, Virginia Governor James S. Gilmore, Former Virginia Governor George Allen, Former President George H. Bush, Chairman of the General Douglas MacArthur Memorial Foundation Roy B. Martin Jr., U.S. Senator John Warner, and Colonel William J. Davis, Marine Corps (retired), executive director of the MacArthur Foundation.

in the April 6 edition of *The Virginian-Pilot.* "Norfolk is honored that he chose this city as the custodian for his papers, memorabilia and final resting place. His name and deeds will be remembered through the years to come." W. Fred Duckworth, president of the MacArthur Memorial Foundation and former mayor, said of the general: "He was considered by many as the world's finest military tactician of the past century, a man of great business ability, an outstanding student of history, and one who above all completely believed in the American way of life."

In the bright sunshine of a spring day in Norfolk, General of the Army Douglas MacArthur was laid to rest with the pomp and ceremony befitting the highest ranking army officer of his day. The preamble to MacArthur's interment on the eleventh included an assemblage of the most preeminent military officers of the century looking on as the procession moved two blocks from the MacArthur Memorial to St. Paul's Episcopal Church, where Attorney General and Mrs. Robert F. Kennedy, representing President Lyndon Johnson, led a roster of official mourners that included prime ministers, ambassadors, governors, admirals, and generals. The general's burial in the city occurred on the thirteenth anniversary of his dismissal as supreme commander of the allied powers in Korea and the Far East, on April 11, 1951, when General MacArthur received a cable from President Truman that he was being returned home. The general's soul was committed to God in a brief religious ceremony in the rotunda of the memorial following lengthy services at St. Paul's. The boom of howitzers firing a nineteen-gun salute and the lonely sound of a bugler playing "Taps" reduced many in the rotunda to tears, including MacArthur's widow, Jean, and their son, Arthur, then only twenty-six years of age. The salute was followed quickly by more prayers and the cracking reports of rifles echoing throughout the square around the memorial.

The General Douglas MacArthur Foundation, which was to use its influence and means to continue supporting what the general had epitomized in life: duty, honor, and country, has flourished since his death. Now over thirty-five years old, the foundation continues its mission to foster scholarship and programs that evoke the spirit and character of MacArthur while the memorial complex, prominently situated at the crossroads of Mile Marker One in downtown Norfolk, hosts tens of thousands of schoolchildren and adult visitors each year.

Roy Martin is pictured on the night he was officially elected with his children, Anne Beverly (left) and Roy B. Martin III. The photograph was taken in September 1962.

CHAPTER 6

Mayor Martin

While perhaps not as heated an issue as integration or annexation, the Norfolk City Council was compelled to ponder a myriad of complex problems in the wake of the reopening of the schools and the hemming in of Norfolk by her new sister cities. In the wake of Massive Resistance and school closures in Norfolk, the tragedy of the "Lost Class of 1959" went on. There was no way to adequately determine how many junior and senior high school students were actually barred from attending school during Virginia's shameful Massive Resistance period and far worse, it was near to impossible to gauge the negative impact to each student's educational preparation. The schools had been open again for nearly three years when *The Virginian-Pilot* editorial of February 14, 1962, remarked that "although a scattering of Negro pupils sit among the whites, classes are conducted pretty much as they were before. *They were suspended,*" the editorial writer noted, "*but a semester: let the dead past lie, say the school-closers and apologists.*" But the editorialist, unwilling to let the apologists off the hook, went on to say that the past was not dead enough. "The tragedy of the lost class not only goes on, it has been enlarged with each succeeding school term and is being compounded yet. For while boys and girls now have schools to attend, they do not have to attend school." Virginia did not have a compulsory school attendance law on the books.

The General Assembly in its special 1959 session repealed the state's compulsory school attendance law in part of Massive Resistance propagators' initiative to be clear of laws that would be breached by the order to close schools. The idea, in truth, was to ensure that if a white child did not want to attend school alongside an African-American child, he or she was not compelled by compulsory attendance laws to do so. Roughly 1,500 students withdrew from Norfolk schools in 1960–61. While some went to work, others entered the armed forces, got married, and others simply "hung out" on the streets and in semipublic places causing trouble. The school dropout rate in Norfolk was better than the Virginia average and considerably higher than the national average, but when studying the issue in depth, the total number of dropouts of children in elementary grades was most alarming. Approximately 290 to 300 children in first through fifth grade had left school. As a direct consequence of Norfolk's juvenile delinquency problem, then Councilman Roy Martin was appointed chairman of the Mayor's Youth Commission to study the problem and proffer solutions. Part of Martin's and the commission's plan

One of the finest programs Roy Martin would begin as a councilman and continue as mayor was a coordinated effort to engage the city's young people in meaningful after-school employment and also provide for recreational centers and libraries that would occupy their time in a positive fashion. The Oakleaf Park Community Center, shown here circa 1958, was one such facility. (Charles S. Borjes, photographer.)

entailed making better use of the city's school buildings and recreational facilities during after-school hours. The commission proposed to the city council, among other programs, that school libraries be kept open longer and school guidance departments be reaffirmed in their importance and expanded, if necessary. In order to curb the youth violence and vandalism that had risen in the wake of young people without enough schooling—or time in school—to know better, the commission urged the formation of trade schools—vocational/technical institutions—and encouraged businesses in Norfolk to extend offers of after-school employment to high-school-age pupils in the city. Working in concert with the Virginia Employment Commission, Martin's plan placed students in jobs for which they were qualified and which exposed young people to job options as graduation or college neared.

Norfolk was not the only community in the nation left with juvenile crime and delinquency issues postintegration, but the city, having begun an aggressive program almost immediately after schools opened again, was on the leading edge of an issue eventually embraced by the nation's president. The problem was so pervasive that then President of the United States John F. Kennedy proposed a five-year federal plan to Congress to combat crime by youth offenders, which extended well beyond the bounds of their juvenile offenses. The Kennedy plan dovetailed the resources of the U.S. Departments of Justice and Health, Education and Welfare. Under the president's Youth Correction Act, the federal government carried on a constructive program to address youth offenders, including investigations by

The clerk of the corporation court, William L. Prieur Jr., swears in Roy Martin, Linwood F. "Cy" Perkins, Edward J. Brickhouse, and Jessie White to the Norfolk City Council on July 18, 1962. (Norfolk Police photograph.)

Newly elected President of the Council Roy B. Martin Jr. (center) posed in September 1962 with his reorganized Norfolk City Council (left to right): Sam T. Barfield, Edward J. Brickhouse, Linwood F. Perkins, Martin, Paul T. Schweitzer, Jessie White, Lewis L. Layton, and City Manager Thomas F. Maxwell.

Attorney General Robert F. Kennedy and Secretary of Health, Education, and Welfare Abraham Ribicoff into causes of youth-based crime.

The Kennedy initiative included, most importantly, a proposal to seek out communities around the country with viable, constructive programs in place to combat juvenile crime and to mold the tenets of the most successful programs into a framework that could be exercised by other municipalities. The president's plan called for

"The mayor's position brings along some entertaining sidelines that have nothing to do with government per se, but are very interesting. For a number of years Norfolk firemen had a Firemen's Band. The evening before Christmas Eve they would come into the neighborhood in front of the mayor's house and play Christmas carols. After Mayor Duckworth retired and I became mayor, they would come to my home and play. All the neighbors would come out and it was a very delightful experience. After they finished playing, I would invite them into the house for a little Christmas spirit, which I'm sure they enjoyed. It was an occasion that reminded me of something that would be held in small communities, not a city the size of Norfolk. As the years went on, the Firemen's Band went out of existence and this was one of the things the mayors were no longer able to enjoy." —Roy B. Martin Jr.

A retirement party was given in honor of former Norfolk Mayor Fred Duckworth (far right) at the Moses Myers House on the corner of Bank and East Freemason Streets on the evening of September 13, 1962. Louise and Roy Martin (standing left) chat with Gertrude and Fred Duckworth as the evening got underway. Fred Duckworth, a man of another era, was born on June 20, 1899, and later met with a tragic end. His wife, born March 16, 1896, died in February 1980.

grants to support pilot programs engaged in such crime-curbing efforts, including juvenile delinquency. With $10 million to expend on pilot programs, Norfolk was recommended for its crime prevention plan and educational initiatives. Particularly attractive to the Kennedy administration was the youth commission's partnership with the city's juvenile court. Judge Edwin A. Henry, of that court, sat on Martin's board. When he became mayor on September 1, 1962, Martin continued the initiative to get a compulsory school attendance law on the books once again—which eventually did occur.

A major test of power loomed as the June 1962 election neared in Norfolk as the city Democratic machine juxtaposed its candidates—most of the incumbent council—against a play by the Citizens for Democratic Government (CDG), a group stumping on the platform it was prepared to take back city governance from the Duckworth team, including Roy Martin. Four of the seven council seats were up for election to four-year terms on June 13, including those belonging to the mayor, N.

Area mayors used to participate in the Annual Soap Box Derby. At first this was held at the amphibious base on the overpass but later moved to Mount Trashmore. Each city had a civic group build a racer for its mayor to race. The city of Norfolk's Junior Chamber of Commerce built Roy's racer. "Needless to say these were very unusual vehicles—nothing like the racers that young people use today in the races." Most of the time, they were made out of boxes, baskets or anything that could put together with a seat and four wheels. "I recall my first race quite well. Mayor Irvine Smith of Portsmouth, who had been mayor for several years and participated regularly in the derbies in years past, told me that I should sit as firmly upright as I could, pushing my back against the seat and holding tight to the steering wheel." The races were run in pairs; two racers were put on a ramp and released at the same time. "It didn't take me very long after I was off the ramp to realize that I had been taken in by Mayor Smith, who happened to be my opponent. In the first race he was hunched over while I was sitting straight up blocking the wind. Mayor Smith was the victor."

"I learned a good lesson there, however, and from that day on I was quite successful in winning the Soap Box Derby. The trophy was a silver-plated oil can that the winning mayor was given at the end of the race. It was passed on from year to year. I won more Soap Box Derby trophies than any other trophies in my life. They were interesting races and we all survived. One day though, one of the mayors lost control of his racer and ran into the side of the ramp! Fortunately, he was not hurt. The races were a lot of fun."

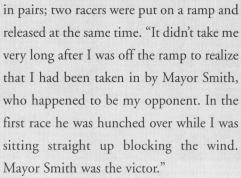

Roy Martin was an avid supporter of the Soap Box Derby for adults and young people. He participated for several years in the competition, winning the Mayor's Tin Can Derby on July 11, 1968 (shown here), at the course set out over the bridge on the Little Creek Amphibious Base running parallel to Shore Drive. Martin is in the racer on the left. He beat Suffolk Mayor James F. Hope.

The USS Missouri returned from a Task Group Forty (TG-40) training exercise in Europe, the only time the battleship ever steamed alongside all three of her Iowa-class sisters—USS Iowa (BB-61), USS New Jersey (BB-62), and USS Wisconsin (BB-64)—and went into Norfolk Naval Shipyard for a major overhaul. This photograph, taken on December 26, 1962, shows the commemorative surrender plaque from Missouri, which had originally been installed aboard ship in October of 1945 by the shipyard's workers to commemorate the battleship's role as the platform for the Japanese surrender on September 2 of that year. Roy Martin is standing on the right. (Official United States Navy photograph.)

B. Etheridge, Martin, and Linwood Perkins. The Citizens for Democratic Government (CDG) had one of its own already on the council: Samuel T. Barfield. While Duckworth, mayor since 1950, was initially reluctant to reveal his intentions to run again, he eventually announced his retirement from city politics. At the same time, N. B. Etheridge, who had been a longtime member of council, also announced he would not be running for reelection due to poor health. Thus, the anticipated departure of Duckworth and Etheridge from city council left Perkins and Martin as the only incumbents seeking election in the upcoming race. "We were able to have two well-known businessmen join us: Jessie White, an insurance executive, and Edward J. Brickhouse, owner of Chesapeake Automobile Supply Company. We had a heated campaign."

The incumbent opposition ran more than a heated contest for city council; it set the stage of political upheaval in Norfolk politics that would extend well past

Martin's career in city governance. William G. Shepheard, the CDG president who had run with Barfield in 1960 and lost his bid for a seat on council by 150 votes, was expected to enter the 1962 contest. Guiding CDG strategy was Henry E. Howell Jr., who had been among four candidates defeated by the Norfolk Democratic regime in a previous primary for state office. The CDG had Howell

Greeting Vice President of the United States Lyndon B. Johnson (center) at a U.S. Conference of Mayors reception for congressional leaders in Washington, D.C., on January 17, 1963, are (left to right): Conference Vice President Arthur L. Selland, mayor of Fresno, California; Mayor Roy B. Martin Jr., of Norfolk, Virginia; and John J. Buckley, mayor of Lawrence, Massachusetts. (United States Conference of Mayors photograph.)

The Public Relations Society of America awarded then Rear Admiral John A. "Jack" McCain Jr. and Norfolk Mayor Roy Martin the association's annual Silver Anvil Award at a dinner held May 17, 1963, at The Waldorf-Astoria Hotel in New York City. The Silver Anvil Award is given to public relations practitioners who have addressed contemporary issues with exemplary professional skill, creativity, and resourcefulness. There are only fifteen categories with only one award given per category and subcategory. McCain and Martin won awards within the government category for armed forces and local governing bodies, respectively.

The visit of President Diosdado P. Macapagal of the Philippines (left facing away) to the MacArthur Memorial on Sunday, October 4, 1964, was commemorated with the presentation by Mayor Martin of a Kenneth Harris print of the memorial. Martin is holding the watercolor on the left and City Councilman "Cy" Perkins is on the right. (Dwain H. Mason, police photographer. Norfolk Police photograph.)

and two other House candidates in primaries, all of whom were unsuccessful. Though local politicians did not then consider Howell a threat and he was not put up for a city council seat, one of his previous running mates was given strong consideration, a woman named Mary W. Thrasher. The CDG had already targeted Duckworth had he opted to run. The group planned to use the mayor's stand on school closing to hurt him in the black polls. By 1962, there were at least five thousand eligible African-American voters in the city.

The election, in the end, proved the team that had been assembled and cultivated for nearly a decade remained strong enough to stave off competition from the CDG and a small Republican-led assault on incumbent councilmen's seats. Martin, Perkins, White, and Brickhouse were each elected to serve four-year terms on the council. At the organizational meeting of the new council, convened in September

Martin attended the twenty-first annual Global Strategy Discussions at the U.S. Naval War College, Newport, Rhode Island, in June of 1969. He is seated to the left of Vice Admiral Richard G. Colbert, a submariner and president of the Naval War College from 1968 to 1971. As a captain, Colbert was the first director of the Naval Command College. When he returned ten years later as president of the war college, he began the first International Seapower Symposium to capitalize on the leadership and diverse perspectives he saw in the representatives of other navies then attending the Naval Command College. Colbert was on the cutting edge his entire career, including his appointment as the eighth commander in chief of U.S. Naval Forces in Southern Europe (CINCSOUTH) on May 31, 1972. Admiral Colbert held the position until relieved by Admiral Stansfield Turner on September 1, 1975. (Naval War College photograph.)

U.S. NAVAL WAR COLLEGE

GLOBAL STRA
16-20 JUNE 1969 N
COM

NEWPORT, RHODE ISLAND

Y DISCUSSIONS
ORT, RHODE ISLAND
TEE 31

Martin poses with Congressman Porter Hardy Jr. (left) and Thomas Downing at a 1967 Charles H. Consolvo Tent Circus Saints and Sinners dinner. The clown statue or "fall guy" is awarded to those who contribute above and beyond the call to community service. Proceeds from the award dinner are donated each year, as was the case here, to a charity of the fall guy's choice.

of that year, Roy was elected president of the council (as is customary) with the honorary title of *mayor*. Linwood Perkins, an old friend and political ally of Martin, was elected to serve as vice mayor. "I assumed the leadership of the city council team because I was probably the most experienced and was knowledgeable of what was going on in the city." In his remarks after assuming the office of mayor, Martin indicated that one of his primary goals was to ensure that each member of council served all the people in Norfolk, refraining, whenever possible, from falling into the "business as usual" character of Norfolk government in the first half of the twentieth century. In particular, Roy wanted to see minorities brought onto city boards and commissions. This had not been the case in the past. The council's first appointment was a prominent African-American lawyer named Hillary Jones, father of Jerrauld R. Jones, an equally prominent attorney and Democrat now active in state politics. The elder Jones became the first black member of the Norfolk School Board. His appointment was followed by a number of others, however, Roy, looking back on that time, remains ambivalent in his response to what was accomplished. "It was a just and very wise decision, but one that never generated any political support among the black community. This was certainly never the intent of these appointments and never deterred council continuing its obligation to see that all citizens were represented on the council."

Roy served twelve years as mayor of Norfolk. "When I reflect back on it, all twelve were very interesting years, but they were also rife with change." During the time Roy served on council, going back to his initial appointment in 1953, the faces on Norfolk City Council evolved with the times. In 1956, Robert F. Ripley chose not to run again and Lewis Layton filled his slot. In 1957, Ezra Summers died suddenly and Linwood Perkins assumed his position. In 1960, George Abbott, who had served as vice mayor for many years, resigned, and his replacement, Paul T. Schweitzer, remained on council until he lost an election in eight years later. Another face who joined the council in 1960, Samuel T. Barfield, ran as an independent and defeated long-term councilman Lawrence Page. Barfield was the first independent to gain a foothold on council. Two years later, in 1962, Duckworth and Etheridge did not run for reelection and in their places Jessie White and Edward Brickhouse were elected. The changes continued in the next election when, in 1964, Lewis Layton retired from council and William P. Ballard filled his slot. When White and Brickhouse decided not to run again in 1966, two new members of council joined the team— Daniel M. Thornton Jr., who ran with Martin, and Robert E. Summers, an independent. Summers was the son of late former councilman Ezra Summers.

The most pivotal election, however, occurred in 1968, the year Joseph A. Jordan Jr. defeated Schweitzer to become the first African American to serve as a member of the Norfolk City Council. Also that year, Bill Ballard died and his position was filled by V. H. "Pooch" Nusbaum Jr., who later served as Martin's vice mayor. A year later, in 1969, Barfield resigned and was replaced by George Hughes, a prominent member of the Norfolk School Board and proactive businessman from Ocean View. Hughes also had a reputation as an outstanding athlete and coach of the city's first stab at a professional football team—the Norfolk Neptunes. R. Braxton Hill, a prominent accountant and business leader was elected to the city council in 1970 along with R. Stanley Hurst, who handily defeated Kenneth Perry who was running as a member of the Martin ticket. Perry's loss was the first serious crack in the Martin team since Roy had become mayor, but more than defeat itself, the election of 1970 was symbolic of more losses and broken alliances to come. When Irvine B. Hill Jr., who had been a Martin supporter, decided to run against Braxton Hill in 1972, he was also running against Martin's handpicked team. While Martin quietly advised Irvine Hill not to run, he did and Braxton Hill was not returned to council in the subsequent election.

Frank A. Dusch, first mayor of the city of Virginia Beach, (left) joined Norfolk Mayor Roy Martin on March 25, 1964, to promote the Norfolk Tour.

CHAPTER 7

Those Bricks-and-Mortar Changes

The bricks-and-mortar changes which occurred while Roy Martin was mayor, some begun when he was still a councilman, remain in large measure his greatest legacy to the city of Norfolk. In a letter Roy composed to then Assistant City Manager James B. Oliver and dated July 29, 1974, he remarked:

> *I think that from the physical change in the city of Norfolk, or as some like to call it—the bricks and mortar—we have shown tremendous accomplishment. We can't overlook the development of the financial district, the opening of Waterside Drive, the new School Administration and Juvenile [and Domestic Relations] Court Building, along with other new schools of which, of course, Booker T. Washington is the largest. The building of Scope and Chrysler Hall, the new Norfolk Regional Airport, new branch libraries, conversion of the old army base terminals into the modern container operation it is today, as well as our suggestion for port unification that finally came about and relieved the city of the financial burden of this facility [are all significant to Norfolk]. The acquisition of the Chrysler collection as well as expansion of the Chrysler Museum [formerly the Norfolk Museum of Arts and Sciences], and certainly if it comes about, one of the greatest inner-city developments in America: Norfolk Gardens.*

While Norfolk Gardens never developed, nearly a quarter century later, the MacArthur Center regional shopping mall was constructed in the sprawling seventeen-acre area that had had, over the decades of Martin's public service, several proposals made for its development. Fortunately, none of those materialized before the city garnered the complex that is there today, one which proudly bears the name of the general who came home to Norfolk under Mayor Duckworth's initial efforts in the early 1960s. But what did materialize during Roy Martin's tenure as mayor reflects what former *Virginian-Pilot* staff writer Don Hunt remarked was "Mayor Martin's leading role in the rebuilding" of the city, "and the concrete evidence is everywhere." Hunt went on to say "the city has changed spectacularly in the past twenty-five years."

The dedication of Norfolk's new City Hall building occurred in the first years of Roy Martin's tenure as mayor of the city. The dedication, held on July 17, 1965, was well attended, drawing an impressive guestlist that included (left to right immediately behind the mayor) Martin (at the podium), Admiral "Whitey" Taylor, then Lieutenant Governor Mills S. Godwin, Second District Congressman Porter Hardy, Admiral Morin, and City Councilman Linwood Perkins. (Norfolk Police Headquarters photograph.)

A general reevaluation of Norfolk's development program and studies leading to the establishment of a comprehensive plan for the city was overdue when Roy Martin broached the city council with the idea to take a hard look at its planning practices—or lack thereof—in the summer of 1961. At that time there was no extant overall plan for the city of Norfolk and there had been no vision for the city's appearance past the redevelopment initiated after World War II. Councilman Sam Barfield was the first to note that the relationships between previously annexed areas of Norfolk County to one another and to neighborhoods that had long been included within the city's downtown boundaries had not been well established. He used Ocean View as his example. Barfield went further to point out the lack of continuity between neighborhoods and the commercial, industrial, and recreational portions of the city. Redevelopment projects often lacked the common thread to make them people friendly. Roy Martin, not yet the mayor, perceived the need to open the topic of Norfolk's discontinuity with his colleagues on city council.

But the discontinuity had become readily apparent before Martin entered the picture. However, bolstered by a well-worded letter to the editor of *The Virginian-Pilot* of July 7, 1961. In the letter, Sheldon J. Leavitt, a Norfolk architect and professional engineer, remarked that each and every decision made on behalf of the city's future, large or small, would be "tortured" without a comprehensive plan in place. "It is rare that a city has the opportunity to recreate for itself a new urban image," he wrote. "The old image which visitors to Norfolk carried away in their memories and snapshots was not a pleasant one. Norfolk shared tawdriness and ugliness and disorganization of plan with the vast majority of American cities but it had none of the urbanities which made those unpleasantnesses tolerable." Leavitt astutely cited the fact that in Norfolk there was no icon section of the downtown to compare with Fisherman's Wharf in San Francisco, no French Quarter, such as New Orleans could claim, no Boston Commons, no Georgetown, no Central Park or Greenwich Village, but most important to his analogy—no Lake Shore Drive, the most important urban thoroughfare in Chicago, Illinois. The image of Norfolk, noted Leavitt, was East Main Street.

"But the most incredible fact of Norfolk's rejection of human values was the lack of public access to the waterfront," observed the well-known and respected architect and engineer. "In this maritime city, the water was—and still is—closed off completely," truncated with the razing of the buildings that once lined little side streets and thoroughfares that fed the water's edge. "Other cities, even the corruptly administered ones, do not," said Leavitt, "find the heart to strip from the people all visual and physical touch with the natural setting." The ramifications of Leavitt's statements were clear: there is more to redevelopment than slum clearance, building highways, and planning cut-throughs to divert traffic from neighborhood streets. "After all," he continued, "cities are for people. If this is recognized, then people will return to them, live in them, work in them, play in them and even spend money in them." Leavitt's well-developed plan was subsequently reaffirmed by an expert brought to Norfolk a couple of months later by Roy Martin.

The foundation for changes, a credit to Martin's foresight, began in the fall of 1961, when he contacted one of the nation's leading urban planners, Dennis O'Harrow, of Chicago, and brought him to the city to study Norfolk's planning methods and recommend changes. "Coordinated planning and development of the city," remarked O'Harrow to a joint meeting of the Norfolk City Council and Planning Commission, "is being unduly subordinated—at least in the eyes of citizens—to the more spectacular accomplishments of redevelopment." He noted further it appeared to him that redevelopment came onto Norfolk's urban landscape to implement municipal plans, noting the city's highway improvements, the razing of slums in the downtown area, and the construction of a new civic center, but in the end, the notion of redevelopment slipped beyond planners' control and usurped the comprehensive planning in which Norfolk needed to be vested. O'Harrow found what he called "a lack of conscious and continuing programs to inform and educate" the public on city planning. He also spotted a need for an official land use plan for the entire city, which then City Planning Engineer Donald Locke was preparing (for the first time) in 1961; an overall economic plan for Norfolk and the region; and a comprehensive plan for recreational uses and schools, cultural institutions, and public spaces. Much of what O'Harrow stated involved what he called an urgent need for long-range studies and plans, inclusive of economic and population studies, zoning, highways and modes of transportation, and cultural resources. "That's what I wanted to hear," stated Martin of the O'Harrow's recommendations in the following day's newspaper.

Reflecting on the brick-and-mortar changes of his past, "One of the things I've always been most proud of," Martin noted, "is the city's role in the development of Old Dominion University." Back in the days when W. Fred Duckworth was mayor and, later, when Roy became mayor, the president of the Norfolk Division of the College of William and Mary, subsequently Old Dominion College—and University—Lewis Webb, would come to the city council meetings and inform the city which parcel of land the college needed for further development. The commonwealth of Virginia was slow to appropriate money for the school, so Webb asked if the council could purchase the property and hold it in trust until the state came up with the funds to buy it. "This we did many times," remarked Martin. The success achieved by Old Dominion University today is testament to the willingness of Norfolk City Council over a span of some forty years to support the institution, which has grown into one of the region's most prestigious centers of higher learning.

Not all of Roy's experiences with bricks-and-mortar changes have been happy ones. Reference has been made on more than one occasion to an incident that occurred during the dedication of the new School Administration and Juvenile and Domestic Relations Court Building. The building, completed while he was mayor, sits at the busy intersection of City Hall Avenue and St. Paul's Boulevard where both roads feed the on-and-off ramps to Interstates 264 and 664. The incident, one that Roy recalls as one of the most disturbing dedications he had ever attended, happened after he had called upon the chief judge of the juvenile court, James V.

Roy addresses the crowd attending the dedication of Norfolk International Terminals on January 20, 1968. Virginia Governor Mills Edwin Godwin Jr. (1966–1970 and 1974–1978) is seated left of the podium.

Martin IV, and left the podium. "We had a large number of people in attendance and it was a celebration we all looked forward to because this was a facility that was badly needed in the city." Unfortunately, the chief judge did not share anyone else's sentiments. He proceeded, his plans unbeknownst to Martin or other members of council, to berate the city of Norfolk for placing the building on such a bustling intersection, arguing that serious accidents and misfortune were sure to be inflicted on citizens trying to traverse the street on their way to the school administration offices and courts. Mayor Martin did not take the remarks kindly and launched into a rebuke of the judge, pointing out that the judge had been party to the building's site plans and had, in fact, approved them. The judge, unfazed by Martin's remarks, held his ground and the event concluded.

The construction of the Scope and Chrysler Hall entertainment complex was one of downtown Norfolk's more significant redevelopment catalysts in the late nineteen sixties. Lawrence M. Cox, then director of Norfolk Redevelopment and Housing Authority, was in Washington, D.C., for a meeting that had been called off, but rather than waste the trip, Cox did some searching through U.S. Housing and Urban Development files and discovered that President Lyndon Johnson had made a commitment to the city of Denver, Colorado, to fund the building of a new convention center as part of the forthcoming 1964 Housing Act. In truth, Johnson had promised a Colorado senator—Peter H. Dominick—his convention center in return for the senator's support on the president's legislation then going through Congress. The convention center amounted to nothing more than big-dollar pork barrel and no one but Cox seemed to know it—at first. Cox immediately called Virginia Senator A. Willis Robertson (father of Christian Broadcasting Network founder Pat Robertson), who contacted the Colorado senator in question to let him know the cat was out of the bag. In a tenor only he could muster, Robertson informed his Senate colleague that if he did not add Norfolk's convention complex to the bill that had cleared the House and was about to go through the Senate on Denver's behalf, Robertson was going to go to the press and expose the senator and Johnson for their scam to get the Denver complex built under the noses of

The Norfolk City Council paused at the groundbreaking of the Scope and Chrysler Hall facility, held on June 6, 1968, for photographer R. V. Fischbeck to preserve the moment for posterity. Council members (left to right) include William Ballard, Paul T. Schweitzer, Linwood F. Perkins, Daniel M. Thornton Jr., Sam T. Barfield, Robert E. Summers, and Roy B. Martin Jr. (Haycox Photographic, Inc.)

American taxpayers. Robertson's subtle, but firm, threat worked; it also opened a plethora of projects to the bill from around the nation, including Hampton, which espied its own convention center along Interstate 64, and Richmond. Cox called Martin at home to explain what he had uncovered, but also to ask a favor. "Larry asked me if we were interested in building a convention center in Norfolk since we had previously drawn up some preliminary plans to expand our arena, a building that held the Center Theater (now the Harrison Opera House) and was only large enough for a basketball game. I told Larry, 'Yes, we were very interested in doing this and we were going to pursue our plans,' to which he replied, 'Well, I'll tell you, if you will announce tomorrow morning that the city of Norfolk is going to build a new arena, I have asked Senator A. Willis Robertson to agree to attach the city of Norfolk to the bill which has cleared the House on Denver and is now before the Senate.'" Cox, aware of the Virginia senator's powerful behind-the-scenes maneuvering, was very confident of success. Porter Hardy, Virginia's Second District congressman, committed his support to the bill when it came to conference.

The same night Cox called Martin, Roy rang City Manager Thomas F. Maxwell and told him what he planned to announce the next day. Maxwell arranged a press conference at ten o'clock in the morning. Martin also asked that all members of the city council be called and informed of Cox's proposal. The manager was instructed to tell councilmen with objections to telephone the mayor at once, but none did. The ball began to roll for what was to become Scope, Chrysler Hall, and the adjacent parking ramp. Cox stayed in Washington for about a week, and through the help of Senator Robertson and Congressman Hardy, the city of Norfolk was allowed to build the convention center as part of its redevelopment program.

"The facility and its financing package never seemed to register with the news media or the public," observed Martin. "A number of Norfolk citizens were opposed to such a project being built because the cost, which included the garage, as well as Scope and Chrysler Hall, amounted to some $33 million. What the public never understood was that it only cost the taxpayers of Norfolk $11 million" due to federal money garnered for Norfolk by Cox and a supportive congressional delegation from Virginia. Since the project was conceived during a council election year, it was labeled "Martin's Mausoleum," a moniker that still brings a wry smile to the former mayor's face.

Lawrence Cox, who was as much a dreamer as driving force in Norfolk's redevelopment years, believed that the city's cultural and convention center should be built by a world-renowned architect. He suggested Pier Luigi Nervi, an Italian architect who was looked upon as the Michelangelo of concrete. Nervi had just finished building a papal center in Vatican City when Norfolk was in its discussion stages of its project. Martin arranged an overseas telephone appointment with Nervi, but the night before he was to place the call, it occurred to Roy that perhaps Nervi did not speak English. An interpreter was dispatched from the office of the Supreme Allied Commander Atlantic (SACLANT) to assist the mayor and city manager with their call. Though Nervi's son spoke some English, Nervi himself did

"This is his day. Looks like everybody's after him today."

—BARFIELD

Willis   Doumar   Burroughs   Martin   Lindsay   Barfield

Criticism Fails to Halt Rome Trip

There are city council meetings which, at least for Martin, he would just as soon forget. One such meeting occurred on November 1, 1966, before his scheduled trip to Rome to meet with Pier Luigi Nervi, the Italian architect hired to design Norfolk's cultural and convention center. At that council meeting, nearly everybody who came to the podium, and including some of Roy's colleagues, chastised the mayor. Those pictured in the Virginian-Pilot *story of November 2, (left to right) were Berry D. Willis, perennial Martin critic, who came to complain about his Rome trip; Norfolk Republican Party Chairman Robert Doumar, who chided Martin for his endorsement of political candidates; William E. Burroughs, a bowling alley operator upset with Roy for not showing up as promised at a tournament; a beleaguered Martin; the elder Harvey Lindsay, one of few who came to Martin's defense; and Councilman Sam T. Barfield, who later observed, "it just wasn't his day" (in reference to Roy's bad day at the helm of council).*

not. After an engaging few moments of pleasantries, Nervi conceded he was interested in undertaking the project in Norfolk and looked forward to receiving further information from the city. The data was forwarded and Nervi subsequently agreed to undertake the design and construction of what is now the Scope complex.

While Nervi made an excellent choice for the cultural and convention center's design, it was decided that the city should use a local architectural firm to do the actual drawings for the project. Despite the choice of Williams and Tazewell to fill that role, Nervi's selection as project consultant stirred constant controversy. E. Bradford Tazewell, along with City Manager Maxwell, Planning Director Philip A. Stedfast, and Mayor Martin made arrangements to visit Rome and meet with Nervi to sign contracts, but even the trip itself drew criticism at city council meetings leading up to Martin's and Stedfast's November 8, 1966 departure. Berry D. Willis, a lawyer and constant critic of Martin's administration, almost immediately began sniping at the mayor's trip. Willis had his supporters—and other issues—perhaps enough to make the November 1 city council meeting one of Roy Martin's worst days in office. While Willis attacked the trip to Rome, Norfolk's Republican Committee chairman, Robert Doumar, rapped Martin for breaching council's nonpartisan political stand by refusing to give Oklahoma Governor Henry Bellmon a police escort when he came to the city in 1965. Roy and the council continued to rebuff the Oklahoma chief of state until the Virginia governor's office intervened. Doumar also cited the mayor's poor treatment of Vice President Richard M. Nixon, who had come to Norfolk later that year, but perhaps Doumar's most indicting attack involved Martin's public endorsement of Harry F. Byrd Jr. and William B. Spong Jr. on October 17, for their U.S. Senate bids. Martin stated unequivocally that he was speaking as an individual, not as mayor, however, the distinction between the two was indiscernible and everyone present in the chambers knew it. Willis, smelling blood in the water, declared "open season on the mayor."6

Roy left Norfolk as scheduled, with a stopover in London for the traditional Lord Mayor's Show, ceremonies inaugurating a new mayor of London, with Stedfast in tow. Maxwell left a day later, but all three officials were to convene in Rome on November 14 for a conference with Nervi. The Norfolk delegation found Nervi a delightful personality, as were his two sons who visited Norfolk a number of times during construction of the buildings.

"We watched, with great anticipation, the development of this unusual building now called Scope," for short, but when it was first built the name was Kaleidoscope, "much too long to pronounce," said Martin. But more to the point, the name fell ran too long for the catchy marketing campaigns envisioned by advertising and marketing firms hired by the city to promote its new crown jewel. Scope became the first building constructed in the United States in over a century that had flying buttresses. "Not only was it difficult to get the design just right, but Norfolk's shallow water table compelled contractors to use a number of pumps to get water out of the foundations," he recalled, thus making the project more difficult than envisioned. At the inauguration of Scope, Roy remarked that the new complex was the city's most significant, "that is," he said more recently, "until the dedication (in 1999) of MacArthur Center."

One of the keys to developing the tourism industry in Norfolk was the creation of the Norfolk Tour by Beverly "Bev" Lawler, president of Lawler Ballard Advertising Agency, in 1962. To better promote the tour, Kenneth Harris, a renowned Norfolk artist, painted watercolors of each of the tour's attractions, which were exhibited at the Norfolk Museum of Arts and Sciences (subsequently the Chrysler Museum of Art), and eventually, Scope, MacArthur Memorial, the Hermitage, the Moses Myers House, and Naval Base Norfolk. The paintings were made into colorful prints to be given as gifts to dignitaries who visited the Norfolk community. "Through the years, I gave many sets of these prints not only to people who visited Norfolk, but when I would go elsewhere to meetings, I took them to present to those that I thought would be interested in our area and its community life."

When the Norfolk Tour began, annual attendance hovered at 108,031, but within five years, the figures leapt to nearly one million. Aside from the tour itself, the city of Norfolk took substantive steps to preserve many of the historical and cultural attractions featured on the Norfolk Tour, an indirect benefit to the droves of visitors the city had begun to draw from outside the Hampton Roads region. Through the years, the Norfolk Tour was the barometer by which Hampton Roads tourism could be gauged. Visitation to the city's eight attractions remained accessible by automobile and chartered bus tours, which made the tour's numbers increase steadily as the years went by, providing the Norfolk with visibility on the national scene that it might otherwise never have captured.

The Norfolk Regional Airport came about because of the increase in air traffic coming into the city of Norfolk. This growth precipitated the construction of more substantive runways to accommodate larger jet aircraft that had replaced smaller and slower progenitors, and hand-in-hand with those changes came the need to build state-of-the-art passenger and cargo terminals.

Through the years, however, the Norfolk Botanical Garden had taken over more and more of the property that was allocated to the airport. Frederick C. "Fred" Huette, then director of parks and recreation for the city, and Wendell L. Winn, chairman of the planning commission and prominent in the nursery business, working together were able to convince the garden clubs, horticulturists, and garden patrons to surrender more of the garden's acreage to the airport for its expected expansion. The city appropriated funds to help move all of the plants that could be transplanted to other areas of the botanical garden so that land could be turned over to the airport. It was through the direct effort of Huette and Winn and planning by the Norfolk Port and Industrial Authority which made it possible for the city to start building what is today Norfolk International Airport.

By 1973, finishing touches had been put on a new $13.5 million passenger terminal and expansion of runways to accommodate larger jet aircraft was complete. Opened in January of the following year, the new terminal complex was the first salvo of a broader plan to enlarge the airport to the specifications that added "international" to its name.

On November 19, 1964, the Department of Defense announced that the United States Army no longer needed its shipping terminal off Hampton Boulevard. The department then turned the facility over to the Maritime Administration on June 30, 1965, which in turn gave it to the General Services Administration for disposal as excess property. By that time, the city of Norfolk was convinced it needed the terminal for its expanding import/export trade. City Manager Maxwell, Martin, Congressman Porter Hardy Jr., and Frederick C. Ray, an assistant city manager, went to work negotiating with the federal government to buy the land. Other federal agencies had been given first dibs; the United States Army, Navy, and Coast Guard each wanted a piece of it, but the city fought to get the property intact. The Army and Navy eventually withdrew their claims, but the Coast Guard tenaciously sought a parcel for a new consolidated Hampton Roads operating base. The city, knowing the General Services Administration's obligation to get the best price for the land regardless of use, persevered. In the spring of 1966, an agreement was worked out and on June 10, General Services Administration returned the property to the Maritime Administration, which had been tasked with a higher obligation to develop American ports and waterborne commerce.

The city of Norfolk acquired the land on July 1, 1966, when the Maritime Administration agreed to lease the facility to the city with thirteen major provisions, including a specification that the city locate a site suitable for a Coast Guard base, to which Norfolk officials readily agreed. A site was subsequently located in the Western Branch borough of Chesapeake and purchased by Norfolk for the Coast Guard.

The conversion of the old United States Army Intermediate Depot into a modern container operation, in addition to Martin's recommendation for port unification that followed, finally came to fruition during his term as mayor, relieving the city of the financial responsibility for sustaining a port operation at the local level. Due to the strength and influence of Congressman Porter Hardy, Norfolk prevailed and bought the land. An appraisal subsequently revealed that it would have been more profitable for the city to develop the property as residential rather than allow it to remain a port terminal, "but this factor was never given a second thought as far as the city council was concerned," said Martin in later years.

The Norfolk Port and Industrial Authority was proactive in the development of the property though, at first, it was turned over to private enterprise to operate. Old Dominion Stevedoring Company, a respected maritime stevedoring company, had been awarded the contract to operate the terminal and they were successful in organizing and developing the port terminal from the outset. However, Old Dominion's owners became increasingly concerned as the Authority edged closer to taking over the operation of the terminal rather than leave it in the hands of an independent operator. After the Norfolk Port and Industrial Authority assumed control, the terminal began to expand because containers had become the shipping method of choice around the world. "At the same time, a group in Portsmouth began a similar facility to Norfolk's and it came to a point where we felt both cities were fighting against one another for business," Martin observed. "Newport News had a smaller terminal than either Portsmouth or Norfolk and was also seeking business for their operation. Later," he continued, "in accepting an award for the city for what we had done to develop the Norfolk International Terminals, I made the comment that I thought it was ridiculous that we were bidding against one another for this type of business and that we really should be interested in just seeing that ships came into Hampton Roads harbor." Roy's presentation at the Virginia Conference on World Trade on October 19, 1967, said pointedly that he thought "there should be one body of control in the port of Hampton Roads." The Virginia State Ports Authority (VSPA) had no power at that time over the Norfolk Port and Industrial Authority, the Portsmouth Port and Industrial Commission, and the Peninsula Ports Authority of Virginia, the agencies charged with the

Secretary of Housing and Urban Development under President Richard M. Nixon, George W. Romney (1969–1973), visited Norfolk on April 14, 1969, to assess the city's progress on issues of redevelopment and quashing the blight that had spread throughout Norfolk's core in the post–World War II era. While on his trip, Romney accepted an invitation to tour the MacArthur Memorial. He is shown here (left foreground) with Jean MacArthur, the general's widow; Lawrence Cox (right of Mrs. MacArthur), director of the Norfolk Redevelopment and Housing Authority; Mayor Martin; and Virginia Governor Linwood Holton (behind Martin). (Millard Arnold, photographer. Norfolk Redevelopment and Housing Authority photograph.)

responsibility of port development within their own communities without regard to what the other cities were doing to increase their share of import/export market. Martin's public call for unification of ports in Hampton Roads was the first by any city official in the region, taking many city-watchers by surprise.

"I will never forget the next morning (after the speech he had given) when I received a call from the chairman of the Norfolk Port and Industrial Authority. He said, 'Roy, what the hell have you done? You've given away the port.'" A proposal from the cities asking for state unification followed not long after Martin's initial remarks.

The commonwealth eventually purchased the cities' terminals under the auspices of the Virginia Port Authority. "Today, I don't know whether, in the long run, it was a financially prudent move for the taxpayers of the city." Unquestionably, the purchase of the terminals was a financial boon to the commonwealth of Virginia because of the tremendous tonnage moving through the port every day. The city of Norfolk, however, derives little taxable income from port traffic and none on the Norfolk International Terminals' vast acreage.

Reelected to the city council in 1966 for fourth full term—his third as mayor—Martin's record of bricks-and-mortar changes included a new civic center, Kirn Memorial Library, expansion of the Norfolk Museum of Arts and Sciences, additions to two municipal hospitals, construction of Lake Taylor High School, planning for expansions to Maury and Booker T. Washington High Schools, and the acquisition of the old Army depot for Norfolk's—and later Virginia's—use as a port facility. The routing of the controversial Waterfront Drive was resolved and work began on the downtown seawall. Likewise, imaginative drawings were made for a cultural and convention center, one of the most expensive public arena projects ever completed in Virginia at that time.

In most of the aforementioned projects, the city council dealt with some form of debate—often with Martin's conduct of meetings blending what one newspaper reporter called "an unpredictable mixture of diplomacy with blunt answers to critics, charm with impatience and good humor with determination."[7] By his own estimation, Martin remarked that his tenure as mayor had had more pluses than minuses. Martin, like his predecessor, had become a driving force in direction the city was to take for many years to come, expunging the notion that the council-manager form of governance makes the mayor weak. While it is true that the city manager runs the administration and council sets the policy in such an arrangement, Norfolk had seen mayors take on administrative roles that breached the rules established by the city charter stating that councilmen could not direct city staff nor, for that matter, dominate them. "Mayor Duckworth rode roughshod over the technicalities for twelve years," wrote Wayne Woodlief of *The Ledger-Star*, "not only whipping councils into line but dabbling in administration as the city built a record for action."[8] Martin left the administration of the city to the manager.

The Norfolk Museum of Arts and Sciences—now the Chrysler Museum of Art—staged an exhibition of Nowlan van Powell's collection of Revolutionary War navy paintings. Here, G. Robert House (left), Norfolk city manager, and Roy Martin converse before the opening gets underway.

In the late 1960s and early 1970s, Roy Martin helped facilitate bringing the art collection of Walter P. Chrysler Jr. to Norfolk. When the Norfolk Museum debuted its Willis Houston Memorial Wing for the press on November 27, 1967, it did so with a good portion of Walter Chrysler's art collection. His Italian and Baroque paintings filled the changing exhibition gallery in the new wing. "This is a place for all the citizens to see," declared Martin. H. Bryan Caldwell, director of the museum, remarked: "We have Mr. Chrysler's paintings downstairs and Mrs. Chrysler's upstairs,"[9] referring to Jean Chrysler's glass collection. Both collections were on indefinite loan to the museum at that time. Virginia Governor Mills E. Godwin Jr. remarked at the wing's official dedication on November 29, noted pointedly for the crowd that "the magnificent new building is a culmination of dreams that go back more than thirty years," adding "the dreams of the men and women who supported and maintained the Norfolk Museum of Arts and Sciences before the cultural explosion, when the arts were woefully lacking in both popularity and prestige."[10] The new wing was designed by the same architectural team that had renovated the old City Hall as General Douglas MacArthur's memorial—William and Geoffrey Platt of New York City—with Finlay F. Ferguson Jr. of Norfolk acting as associate architect. The cost was $1.2 million. The E. T. Gresham Company did the actual construction work. Guests for the dedication dinner, however, included the ever-observant Walter P. Chrysler Jr. and his Norfolk-born-and-raised wife, Jean, both of whom had placed art collections on long-term loan to the museum. Little did anyone realize, Martin included, that Chrysler was beginning to want for a more permanent repository of his entire art collection.

"Fortunately, Jean Outland Chrysler, Walter's wife, and I had gone to school together. I received a call one day [some time later] from Jean telling me that Walter was looking for a more permanent home for his vast collection. Since he felt the Chrysler family had an unpleasant history of dying in their early sixties and he was turning sixty, Walter wanted to know if we were interested in having his collection reside in what was then the Norfolk Museum of Arts and Sciences. Without hesitation," Martin continued, "I said 'of course we were interested.'"

Chrysler was delighted by Martin's response and soon came to Norfolk on what would be several visits preliminary to placing the collection here permanently. On his first visit, Chrysler met with fifteen of Norfolk's arts and community leaders, including members of the Norfolk museum's board of directors, to state his proposal for their comment. The plan, as he laid it out, was to draw an agreement that would include changing the name of the Norfolk Museum of Arts and Sciences to the Chrysler Museum and also that the city would add a wing to the existing edifice costing at least $1 million. This addition was necessary in large part due to the vast art glass collection belonging to Jean Chrysler as well as Walter's art, purportedly valued between $65 and $80 million at the time his offer was made to the city.

The day Chrysler arrived in Norfolk, Roy took him to meet with City Manager Maxwell. In the course of their conversation, and with ongoing construction of the Scope complex, including its unnamed concert hall, hammering away in the background, Maxwell, without warning, made a remark to Chrysler that floored his mayor. "You know, Mr. Chrysler, I believe that council will be very happy to name that new theater Chrysler Hall." A bemused Martin later commented: "That is how we ended up with Chrysler Hall and also the Chrysler Theater at the Chrysler Museum of Art. Needless to say, you could almost have picked me up off the floor when his suggestion was made, but Walter grasped hold of the idea so quickly, he beamed from ear to ear." While Chrysler beamed all day at the name changes in his honor, Martin was well aware that the name changes, especially that of the Norfolk Museum of Arts and Sciences, would not leave those in charge of the museum with smiling faces. As he would note at the time—and years later—it was akin to taking away "their private club," referring to the leadership of the museum, whose chairman of the board, William L. "Billy" Parker, who had affectionately been called "Judge" Parker since childhood, was far from enamored—or impressed—with Walter Chrysler. And, in all fairness, Parker was not alone.

Chrysler made a good presentation to the museum and city council, often noting the worth of his collection, but he also broached, perhaps too often for the museum board's taste, his plans for what should be done to the museum to accommodate the art, including the name change, construction of wings, and subjects, which in general terms, put Parker and company on the defensive. From the first presentation in Norfolk to follow-on appraisals and inspections by museum board members, the process did much to expose the growing animosity between Chrysler and the Parker-led board. The acquisition in jeopardy, Martin called a press conference following one of Chrysler's key presentations to the city so that the value of his gift and the public's excitement righted the process and brought some stability to negotiations. Parker and a handful of his board objected strongly to Martin's press conference. Three of them, including Parker, took the city to court to stop the name change, but were unsuccessful. While the lawsuit crashed and burned on arrival, the schism it opened in the arts community, especially after Chrysler moved with his collection to Norfolk, lingered for years to come.

In 1971, the Norfolk Museum of Arts and Sciences merged with the Chrysler Museum in Provincetown, Massachusetts, and was thereafter known as the Chrysler Museum at Norfolk (later changed to the Chrysler Museum of Art. With the consolidation came Jean Outland Chrysler's 7,500-piece glass collection and Walter's complete art collection, including an archive of musical instruments that were housed in a separate house museum on Yarmouth Street, within a short walking distance of the Chrysler. The fallout from the name change, however, had an immediate impact on the museum itself. H. Brian Caldwell quit in protest and Parker was eventually removed as board chairman.

Through the years, the value of Walter Chrysler's collection as part of the whole museum's holdings has grown astronomically, but so has the collection held by the museum prior to Chrysler's donation. The art of William and Florence Knapp Sloane was equally extensive—and valuable, and was one of the examples used by Chrysler opponents to justify the reason for not naming the museum for him alone. Although Walter Chrysler died on September 17, 1988, before the completion of museum additions he had requested, he knew the city had the project underway. A number of years later the city renovated the entire museum, thus making it the first-class facility it is today. Roy served in the early 1990s as president of the Chrysler board of trustees.

Norfolk, which began its redevelopment program after World War II, continued to pursue aggressive renewal projects throughout Martin's tenure on city council and as mayor. The U.S. Department of Housing and Urban Development (HUD) recognized Norfolk's program as one of the best in the nation. "Seldom did a week go by that we didn't have visitors from other communities come to see just what we were doing in the city. There is no question that some people were hurt by our redevelopment programs, however, it took cleaning out some of the worst slums in Virginia to give us the land to develop projects such as the City Hall complex, Scope, Chrysler Hall, the Golden Triangle Hotel and many other projects," Martin is quick to point out. As the years went by, the waterfront, too, began to be redeveloped and "before I left office, we were in the process of seeing much of Ghent razed where Sentara Norfolk General Hospital and Eastern Virginia Medical School are today as well as the start of clearing the area that is now East Ghent."

Redevelopment in Norfolk was piggybacked with funding from entities such as the Model City program, one of the most extensive federal programs in which the city became involved in the late sixties and seventies. Over two hundred American cities applied to participate in the program, but Norfolk emerged as one of only sixty-three that were chosen. The success of Norfolk's application to the Model City program followed on the heels of the city's first coup years before when Norfolk had the distinction of being named an All-America City. The basic objective of the Model City initiative, as well as designation as an All-America City and a broad spectrum of Norfolk's redevelopment programs, was essentially the same— to improve the quality of life for people residing in the city's corporate boundary. The area of Norfolk which participated in the Model City program was a crescent-shaped area around downtown Norfolk that included Berkley, Campostella, Brambleton, Huntersville, and East Ghent. The federal government put up the funds to provide, across the board, coordinated attacks on blight and social service requirements in the core metropolitan area.

Norfolk's plan was sculpted by Norfolk Redevelopment and Housing Authority and in its first year, received $11 million from HUD to begin implementation of the program as it had been outlined to the federal government. "When I reflect on the Model City program," said Martin, "I realize that it did have many advantages and successes. In other cases, I felt that possibly the money could have been better spent in other ways than on some of the programs initiated by the Model City committees that were established in the various neighborhoods. The fact remains, it was a program that pumped a great deal of additional

After completion of Scope and the Chrysler Hall complex, Roy fashioned his official Christmas card and proudly used the image of the city's cultural and convention center on the face of his mayor's greeting card to promote the facility.

money into the city for which we're thankful to have been a recipient." The Model City program was subsequently phased out in favor of federal revenue sharing, the first year of which ended in 1973.

The expansion of the Norfolk Zoo (today the Virginia Zoo) was yet another important investment in the cultural life of the city. "The idea of expansion came about by my attending a meeting of the U.S. Conference of Mayors. Louise was along with me and happened to be talking to the wife of the mayor of Syracuse, New York, a former Norfolk resident who had attended the same elementary school as my wife—the Meadowbrook School," Roy recounted. As the conversation progressed, Louise Martin soon learned that the woman's father owned a carnival, Strates Shows, one of the largest carnivals in the United States, which traveled by railroad and wintered at what is now the Norfolk International Terminals. Several years later, the woman's brother, James Strates, managed the carnival on a trip back to Norfolk that had been underwritten by a local sponsor. Strates invited the mayor to come out to the carnival grounds with his children. Roy later described Strates as "a delightful person. He was obviously a very good businessman and well educated."

The carnival returned to Norfolk in May 1970 and Jim Strates called Roy to ask whether the city had a zoo. "I, being honest," said to Strates, 'Yes we do have a zoo.' Of course, I didn't go into the details of what the zoo entailed at the time. It was basically some alligators, a black bear, a few monkeys and a bison." Strates informed Martin that he had two elephants—Mona and Alice—that no longer performed and he did not need them to help move equipment. He asked if the Norfolk Zoo would like to have the pachyderms. "I immediately accepted the gift and arranged to have them delivered to City Hall the next day so we could take some pictures. When I called City Manager Maxwell and told him that I had received a gift for the city, he was thrilled," that is, until he heard that the gift was two over-the-hill—and rotund—carnival performers named Mona and Alice.

The elephants were housed in an enclosure where they, along with rhinoceroses and hippopotamuses are kept today. This gift was the modest beginning of what exists at the present-day Virginia Zoo. "One of the things that amazes me," Martin observed, "is we had criticism for what we did with Walter Chrysler, we had criticism for what we did with Scope, we had criticism for putting money into the MacArthur Memorial, but I never recall one complaint letter to the editorial page of the newspaper, nor a letter to the mayor's office or from any source complaining about the $265,000 put into a new facility for the elephants, which goes to show that the people of Norfolk do want a good zoo."

Norfolkians also wanted good sports venues, even in the days when Roy Martin was mayor and beyond that, to the time when he was a fledgling city councilman. The desire for an adequate stadium to attract a major league farm team to fill the stands harked back to the heyday of the Norfolk Tars, who drew tens of thousands of onlookers to their field near the center of town. Metropolitan "Met" Park, was, in its day, looked upon as one of the most modern minor league parks in the United States, much like Harbor Park is today. The concept for Met Park was originally proposed to the city by a newspaper sports editor, George McClelland, who had contacts with the New York Mets and knew the club was interested in having a farm team and new park here. The new ballpark would be paid for by the New York Mets organization over a twenty-year lease. At the end of twenty years, the park was paid off. The city gained an excellent farm team and a fine baseball facility for its day, both of which might never have come to pass without the seed money Norfolk provided to jump-start construction of the original park facility.

Unequivocally one of the most lasting and important brick and mortar changes to occur while Roy Martin was mayor is Eastern Virginia Medical School, founded in 1973. The idea for a medical school in the Norfolk originated with a suggestion made at the dedication of the Medical Tower on January 14, 1961, a towering medical office building at the intersection of Colley and Brambleton Avenues. Lawrence M. Cox, the city's venerable housing and redevelopment director, in making remarks that afternoon, brought out the point that building the new Medical Tower adjacent to Norfolk General Hospital was the proper place for establishment of a medical college in a city that "is at the center of one of the largest metropolitan areas in the nation without a medical college. He cited the existing hospitals and clinical facilities in Norfolk as the medical "'nuclei' of which a medical college would be the logical corollary." At a council meeting in January 1961, before Martin was mayor, he picked up on what Cox had suggested and asked the city manager to study the feasibility of such a facility being developed. "At that time, the *Virginian Pilot*'s editorial page noted that my idea was 'a well-timed suggestion.'"

But starting a medical school from the foundation up posed several problems that required intense analysis—and perseverance. Physicians had to be willing and qualified to teach and the most difficult challenge, from a practical standpoint, would be assembling a teaching faculty. The latter problem was far from insurmountable, however. The national statistics at the time noted a longstanding physician shortage. Medical schools in the United States graduated fewer than 7,000 doctors a year at that time, with hospitals trying to fill 11,500 internships annually. The shortfall was inordinately lopsided. Norfolk had its own shortage of physicians to meet the needs of a burgeoning regional population. Some of Norfolk's leading civic leaders had already pondered the shortfall and concluded it was time to establish a medical college in connection with the medical center expanding on the Medical Tower/Norfolk General Hospital site.

The medical-school concept continued to be studied and researched, and in April of 1963, two years after Martin originally asked the manager to prepare a report detailing what it would take to establish a medical school in the city, one particular idea took hold that would move the "concept" closer to reality. Martin, now mayor, listened. Dr. John Thiemeyer, then president of the Medical Society of Norfolk, that a mayor's committee be formed to study and to harness possible support toward developing a medical school in the city. "I followed the suggestion with an appointment of the committee. During this period, Dr. Mason Cooke Andrews, who became such a key proponent of the institution, convinced me of the importance of this institution. I was able to get the city manager and the council to appropriate seed money" in the amount of $100,000 per year—a sum that later climbed to half a million—to assist medical school planning initiatives.

In January 1964, the Norfolk City Council asked the Virginia General Assembly for legislation to establish a Norfolk Area Medical Center Authority. The medical authority was conceived to advance planning—and the following establishment—of the school. In April of that year, the Virginia legislature established the authority and the city appointed a seven-member Medical Center Authority board. Two years later, in October 1966, the council voted to extend the area for the Norfolk Area Medical Center to 17.69 acres in the Ghent section of town to accommodate what was then projected to be a $100-million medical industry in the heart of the city. After the vote was taken by the council, Martin remarked for the record: "I hope no one will feel in years to come that a mistake was made here today."

The plan of the Norfolk Area Medical Authority, endorsed by the Norfolk Redevelopment and Housing Authority and the Norfolk Planning Commission,

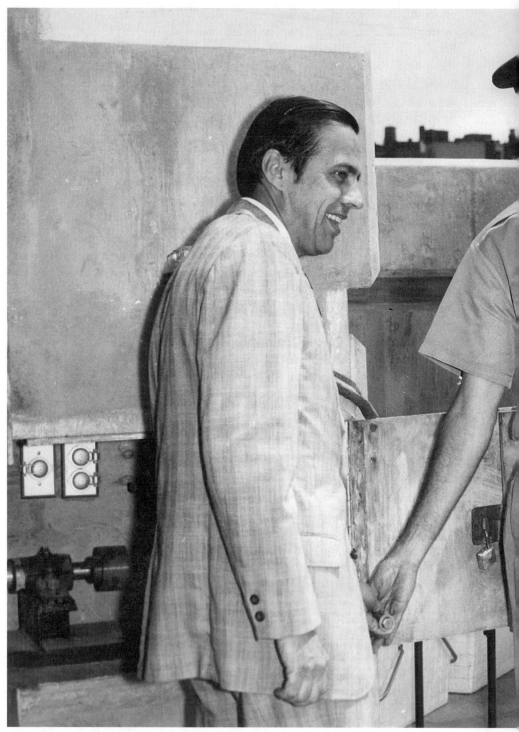

Norfolk Mayor Roy Martin and Colonel James H. Tormey, Norfolk District Engineer, U.S. Army Corps of Engineers, dedicate the Norfolk floodwall on June 8, 1971.

called for the expansion of future medical school grounds into a seven-block area of Ghent, including most of that community's largest commercial corridor at that time. Colley Avenue was rerouted along an area beginning near Pembroke Towers and ending near the present-day intersection of Redgate and Colley Avenues. All the land to the west of the new Colley Avenue was taken up by the center. Roughly 165 landowners were impacted by the proposed medical center plan that swung Colley eastward. But the city council vote was unanimous. "Studies have convinced us that elements of the center can function effectively only if not fragmented by traffic,"[11] said Dr. Mason Andrews, the authority chairman, to a standing-room-only crowd in council chambers.

Among those speaking in favor of the medical center expansion was Frank Batten, rector of Old Dominion College, which had previously agreed to affiliate but not enjoin with the medical school that would be part of the center. "The only hope for fulfillment of a medical school was to locate it in the medical center. It is the only way we can foresee realization of a medical school in Norfolk."[12] Samuel Ames, president of the Norfolk Chamber of Commerce, reiterated what had been said by the majority of speakers at the council podium, when he remarked that the center would be a tremendous asset not only to Norfolk but the entire region. Of those who might lose their homes and businesses to the expansion, Ames said "the good of the greatest number must take precedence over an individual even where his own home is involved."[13]

"When I reflect on the medical school, I feel that the city of Norfolk has been overlooked in helping to establish this college," said Martin. "If it had not been for the city's seed money, I believe those who were key players in the planning and eventual establishment of the school, would readily admit that it would have taken several years more to get the project off the ground," had it not been for the infusion of capital approved by the city council. "There again," he continued, "it was an example of the council taking a chance which has accrued to the benefit not only of the citizens of Norfolk but, unquestionably, all those living in this part of the commonwealth and northeastern North Carolina.

Vice President of the United States Hubert H. Humphrey visited Norfolk to attend the Civic Club luncheon in honor of the 1965 Azalea Festival on April 22, 1965. The event took the vice president from his arrival at Naval Air Station Norfolk to the MacArthur Memorial, with a stop for lunch at the Golden Triangle Hotel in between. Vice President Humphrey is shown shortly after his arrival at the naval air station on Air Force Two. The admiral following Humphrey and his Marine Corps escort is Admiral H. Page Smith. (Official United States Navy photograph.)

Only Two Things Are Sure—
Water and Taxes

olitical hot potatoes continued to be tossed between Norfolk and Virginia Beach after the town of Virginia Beach merged with Princess Anne County to form that city in 1963, not the least—and perhaps the most enduring—of which centered on the water supply. Several times Roy Martin met with Sidney Kellam, who had taken a dominant leadership role in Virginia Beach politics, to discuss water agreements, including possible mergers, to no avail. During his meetings with Kellam, Roy continued to prod his politically adept counterpart about the continued need for unification of the two cities, to which Kellam nearly always replied the same, his arm around Martin's shoulders: "Roy, I think there's a possibility about this and I'm going back and talk to my boys about it." Of course, Martin never heard another word on the subject from Kellam, but whenever an election came up in Virginia Beach, Norfolk's refusal to enter into a compact with the Beach over water was always one of the issues voiced loudest by voters.

There was a tentative agreement reached seven years later, in 1970, between then city manager of Norfolk, Thomas F. Maxwell, and Virginia Beach City Manager Roger Scott whereby the two agreed to set up a water commission for the two cities. However, the commission never materialized for two reasons. One, neither manager could spell out whether it should be a water commission or a water and refuse commission. And second, before the matter could be brought to the city council in Norfolk, Maxwell resigned from office. Maxwell's successor, G. Robert House, came to Norfolk from Chesapeake where he had just begun a water system. "Bob felt that every community should control its water system and he was not anxious to see this agreement between Virginia Beach and Norfolk enacted. It never came up again during my remaining years on council."

Next to the water battles with Virginia Beach, the sales tax issue in 1964 played a starring role, a place in the city's history which Roy could still recall, decades later, as one of the most difficult of his tenure as mayor. The city, like all cities and counties in Virginia, was pressed for ways to raise additional revenue other than repeatedly turning to real estate or personal property taxes, both of which typically drew negative voter response at the polls if increased or their matrix altered in any way.

City Manager Maxwell had devised a program in late 1963 to charge a 2 percent sales tax with the stipulation made that it could not exceed four dollars on any one item purchased. From the outset, Norfolk drew support from neighboring cities to go ahead with the sales tax program, but as time went on and "politics being what they are," Roy related, "we found an avalanche of criticism, particularly from the merchants and the business community to the new program." Once stalwart support

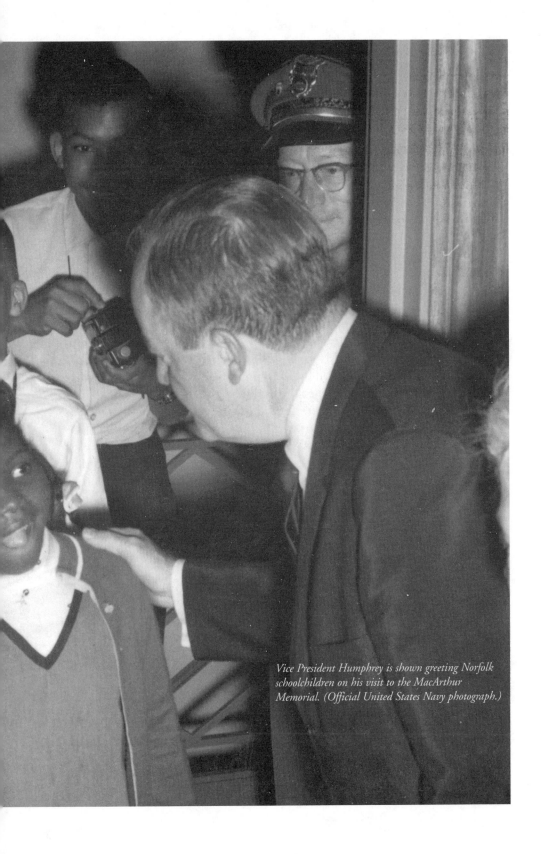

Vice President Humphrey is shown greeting Norfolk schoolchildren on his visit to the MacArthur Memorial. (Official United States Navy photograph.)

from Hampton Roads municipalities ebbed quickly when criticism of Norfolk's plan reached fever pitch in the press.

"This was the only time in my political career that I was ever threatened. I was threatened by one of my better customers who said that he would no longer maintain any of the products I marketed on his shelves if I pursued the sales tax." Threats to Martin's food brokerage business swiftly became secondary to the onslaught of negative press and the opposition of the Norfolk Redevelopment and Housing Authority to the proposed sales tax. Martin took the housing authority's lack of support for the tax rather personally, an agency he had noted on more than one occasion, "we supported all the way down the line," but "which turned against us." There was little substantive support for the sales tax, yet Norfolk needed a revenue stream to keep public projects financially viable.

The city, despite a decided lack of support from other cities and Norfolk Redevelopment and Housing Authority, opted to enact the sales tax for a budgetary period of six months to test the waters. "It was very difficult for me to keep the majority of city council in support of the program, but it won on a 6 to 1 vote. Fortunately, the sales tax did not drive any business from the city and proved, in the end, to provide a respectable windfall to city coffers." Unfortunately, the commonwealth of Virginia watched Norfolk incubate the sales tax program and saw the money it generated—multiplied by every municipality in the state—a far more appealing prospect. At the next General Assembly session, state legislators stripped individual cities and counties of their right to charge a sales tax. In its place, the General Assembly enacted a program in which only a portion of state sales tax returns to localities. "Although it was a very difficult undertaking and the state took over the program, I feel if we had not done what we did, the state would probably have allocated very little money back to the cities. I think the people of Norfolk should be praised for not going against the tax. In the end, the man on the street did not seem to object to the sales tax as much as the business leaders in the community. I must say that after it proved its success, many of those who were opposed to it, including the newspapers, came around and said we were right."

The lack of regional cooperation on the sales tax initiative forwarded by Norfolk pointed to the deepening divide among Hampton Roads cities, none of whom could afford to ignore opportunities to the benefit of their citizens or fail to identify initiatives detrimental to the same. As mayor of Norfolk, Roy came up with a group known as the Area Wide Committee on Cooperation, similar in nature to the contemporary Mayors and Chairs forum. "I conceived the idea of having the mayors of our sister cities, joined by one citizen of each mayor's locality, join me for an initial get-together in Norfolk to discuss area-wide matters concerning the municipalities. The cities joining Norfolk were Chesapeake, Virginia Beach, Portsmouth, Suffolk, Hampton, and Newport News. The first meeting got off to a shaky start when the Virginia Beach representative brought up the question of water. Before the representative could finish his remarks, the Suffolk mayor responded that if this meeting was turning into a fight between Norfolk and Virginia Beach over water, then Suffolk and the other cities didn't want any part of it. The Virginia Beach representative immediately withdrew his remarks." From that day in 1963 on, the cities met quarterly—and cordially—to discuss pertinent subjects until the committee stopped meeting in the late 1970s.

Other than discussions held during Area Wide Committee on Cooperation meetings, the Hampton Roads cities' mayors and state legislators got together before each session of the General Assembly to make a "wish list." Each community would list what they would like the General Assembly to consider, and once the listed was complete, it was passed among all the cities for summary review. Any item on the list that an individual city did not approve or did not want considered was automatically eliminated. The list started with as many as eighty or ninety items but could end up with as few as fifteen. Whatever remained on the list went to the General Assembly.

Vice President Humphrey was accompanied on his trip to Norfolk by his wife, Muriel Humphrey. Norfolk Mayor Roy Martin is to their right. The picture was taken as the official party entered the ballroom of the Golden Triangle for lunch. (Official United States Navy photograph.)

Mayor Martin (far right) makes conversation with (left to right) actor Dan Blocker, Second District Congressman Porter Hardy (1947–1969), and Virginia Governor Albertis Sydney Harrison Jr. (1962–1966) at the Azalea Festival dinner on April 24, 1965. Blocker played Hoss Cartwright on NBC-TV's popular "Bonanza" until he died on May 13, 1972, months shy of his forty-fourth birthday. (WAVY AM/TV photograph.)

CHAPTER 9

Campaigns of Personality

Roy Martin returned to Norfolk after a war that left it a dilapidated port city full to the brim with slums, brothels, and bars. In his—and the so-called Martin team's—zeal to change the downtown Norfolk landscape, the campaigns of personality began. Throughout the 1950s and 1960s, W. Fred Duckworth and his able successor, Martin, formed the foundation of the silk-stocking group which ran the city with little opposition. In many respects, if you did not agree with Duckworth or Martin, you left town. There was no alternative. But like most stories, there are two sides. There is what he has accomplished, "clearly those brick-and-mortar accomplishments represented jobs, education, and culture,"[14] as former Norfolk Mayor and School Board Chairman Vincent J. Thomas has said, but the other side of the story is how he did it.

Samuel Ames, then president of the Norfolk Chamber of Commerce, said of Roy after his reelection to council in 1966—his fourth full term and third election as mayor—that his success or failure boiled down to strong, aggressive personality. "I don't think anybody can deny that the [Martin] years have been good. I think Roy is his own worst enemy from the public relations standpoint. He's blunt. And yet you always know where you stand with him. He's spent much more time being a councilman than the job calls for. I don't see how he can do it and run his own business, too."[15] Roy's notoriety and influence went far outside the city of Norfolk. Back in the mid-sixties, he was one of only fifteen mayors on the executive committee of the National League of Cities, an urban research and congressional lobbying organization that represented 350 major cities and some 14,000 municipalities nationwide. His work on the National League of Cities sent his star soaring. Thomas Chisman, then the immediate past chairman of the committee, remarked to a reporter in September 1966 that he was convinced all cities could use more Roy Martins. William Sauder, an astute and well-respected urban affairs reporter for *The Richmond News Leader* and former *Virginian-Pilot* staff writer, said Martin was "the hard, tough knot who held council together"[16] during the battle to pass the sales tax initiative. "Roy's biggest weakness, and the only thing that stands between him being a great mayor," continued Sauder, "is his instinctive disposition to be short with people who disagree with him. I don't think it's a fatal weakness. He's a strong, progressive mayor."[17]

Roy was progressive enough to continue on the path of minority appointments he had promised when he took the mayor's office in 1962, but this, too, often proved a double-edge sword. The city council chose a black publisher named Thomas W.

Study Group Reactivated

Beach to Fight Annex Plan

By MORRIS ROWE
Virginian-Pilot Staff Writer

VIRGINIA BEACH — Sidney S. Kellam, fearing what he said could be a takeover of Virginia Beach by Norfolk, asked the City Council Monday to fight annexation-law changes proposed last week by Norfolk Mayor Roy B. Martin Jr.

The council "reactivated" the city's old Consolidation Study Commission and passed a resolution supporting Kellam's denunciation of Martin's plan for an-nexation by commission rather than courts.

Kellam's Organization, represented by candidates of the Administration Team, is fighting in a primary battle with the United Candidates, headed by a former Kellam lieutenant, City Treasurer V. A. (Jack) Etheridge.

Etheridge called Kellam's rare appearance before the council "a cheap attempt to reap publicity through the council."

United House of Delegates candidate B. R. Middleton in a statement branded Kellam's action "another desperate attempt to help his fading organization."

In a hearing before the Virginia Metropolitan Areas Study Commission, Martin had proposed that a newly created State Division of Planning be empowered to recommend annexations.

The recommendation would then be reviewed by a special commission. A three-member panel of judges decides annexation cases in the present system.

The council deviated from its agenda at the request of City Manager W. Russell Hatchett to "permit the Honorable Mr. Sidney S. Kellam to address" the

council on a matter of what he termed "grave importance."

Kellam recalled the early annexation fight with Norfolk which in turn caused the formation of the Consolidation Study Commission of 11 men to merge Princess Anne County and the small resort city of Virginia Beach.

The merger was worked out between September 1961 and the date the two subdivisions became one, Jan. 1, 1963.

The commission advertised and promoted merger as a measure to keep any more of the city from being annexed by

Kellam

Waving a cautionary hand at Norfolk's proposal to merge was Virginia Beach political boss Sidney S. Kellam, who was vehemently opposed to Martin's plan. The photograph and article ran in the June 13, 1967 Virginian-Pilot.

Young, who along with attorney Victor J. Ashe started the Goldenrod ballot in black districts in the late 1950s, as the first African American named to the Norfolk Redevelopment and Housing Authority board of commissioners. The date was May 15, 1967. Councilman Robert E. Summers refused to vote yes to Young's appointment, causing a rift on council that led to heated discussion between Martin and his colleague more so because Roy expected a 7 to 0 decision than a disagreement. He also clearly wanted the selection process to wrap up quickly, citing a prolonged process that could conceivably lead to more of what he called "campaigning" for other candidates. Aside from the delay, what had not been said aloud was all too clear—the powerful implications that Young's appointment held for Martin's administration. A minority appointment by Martin was crucial to the upcoming council election in which a strong black candidate was running against three incumbents, one of whom—Schweitzer—was most vulnerable to being unseated. Martin needed to protect the team ticket.

Within a month of the council's appointment of Young, Martin called the senior member of the Norfolk School Board, Constance Griffin, his longtime critic and an eight-year veteran of the board, to thank her for her service. "That's how it's done here," she would say later, noting the mayor did not tell her directly that she was not reappointed. The fact Griffin was not reappointed was read two ways. One faction thought it was retribution for her being a thorn in the council's—particularly the mayor's—side for so long, but others, including the print media at that time, viewed her departure as a routine rotation of board members, which, in truth, it had been. Martin had earlier stated that it was time to revamp the city's boards and commissions, bringing aboard new blood and ideas to invigorate Norfolk's various organizations. In Griffin's place, Roy appointed the daughter-in-law of reform mayor John

Twohy II, a critical member of the Cooke-Darden-Twohy team who had set the city on its postwar course. Margaret Twohy, mother of six girls, proved an able member of the school board.

A campaign of personality—of a different kind—had continued over the years between Martin and Virginia Beach political boss Sidney S. Kellam. The subject was always the same—annexation. Unable to accept Norfolk's landlocked status, Roy continued to probe Virginia Beach Mayor Frank A. Dusch for a chink in his armor that might indicate he might be amenable to a merger of the two municipalities. Martin proposed to the Virginia Metropolitan Areas Study Commission on June 6, 1967, which called for revamping the state's annexation procedures. His proposal called for abolition of the annexation process as it existed and aimed to create a state commission to consider annexations presented by the newly formed State Division of Planning. In other words, Martin was proposing annexation by commission rather than the courts, specifically a three-judge panel that had in past ruled against Norfolk when it lost a bid to annex parts of Princess Anne County and Norfolk County in 1962. Norfolk State Delegate John R. Sears Jr., while not opposed to what Martin had to say, suggested the state create a boundary commission to study the issues and understand the implications for all Virginia municipalities. When Sidney Kellam got wind of Martin's proposal, and fearing a takeover by Norfolk, asked Dusch for the floor of the Virginia Beach City Council

Martin Disappointed

Dusch Says No to Talks On Merging

By BILL McALLISTER

Virginian-Pilot Staff Writer

N O R F O L K—Virginia Beach Mayor Frank A. Dusch Thursday rejected Mayor Roy B. Martin Jr.'s call for consolidation talks between their cities. "I have not found any sentiment among the council or among the people of our city who feel that we should seriously take this matter under consideration," Dusch said in a letter to Martin.

"I have not found any sentiment among the council or among the people of our city who feel that we should seriously take this matter under consideration."

Virginia Beach Mayor Frank A. Dusch rebuffed Roy Martin's merger talks on June 16, 1967. This headline from the next day's Virginian-Pilot *clearly expressed the sentiment of those living in the resort city.*

meeting of June 13. He called upon the council to fight annexation by commission as proposed by Martin. "A commission," Kellam said would, "bring about such ill feelings among the people that it would, in my opinion, end metropolitan cooperation among our communities."[18]

There was nearly always some dispute between Martin and Kellam. The running battle of two strong—and politically powerful—personalities provided colorful chapters in both Norfolk and Virginia Beach council histories. The annexation-by-commission dispute grew out of Martin's presentation to the state's area study commission in which Roy implied the South Hampton Roads communities were fortunate to have eliminated "tensions" surrounding annexation cases. He went on to say that Norfolk "does not consider its inability to expand its territory an asset, but rather a major problem of this core city,"[19] which it continued to be. The relationship

Martin, Barfield Spar Over Welfare 'Probe'

By BILL McALLISTER
Virginian-Pilot Staff Writer

NORFOLK — Mayor Roy B. Martin Jr. and City Councilman Sam T. Barfield argued vigorously Tuesday over the findings of Barfield's "own little investigation" of the city Welfare Department.

The mayor accused Barfield of attempting to undermine efforts the council has already put in motion to get the state to take over the local welfare programs.

Those efforts, Barfield countered, are not being pursued actively enough. He sought and won from the council a resolution asking the state for the takeover and asking the matter to be brought before a state meeting of city officials here next month.

The exchange between Martin and Barfield—a rarity for a public meeting of the council—lasted nearly 10 minutes.

It had its antecedents in a less-heated exchange two week earlier when Barfield questioned whether there was any way the city could purge its welfare rolls. Martin then said he didn't understand what Barfield's point was and suggested he read reports that had been furnished councilmen.

At one point Tuesday Martin accused Barfield of "pulling the rug" from under City Manager Thomas F. Maxwell, who has long been an advocate of greater

"This idea (state operation of city welfare programs) came from council and has been pursued vigorously."

—Martin

"It hasn't been done,"
. —Barfield

state aid for local welfare programs.

The exchange began as Barfield reported on conversations he had had with Maxwell, the head of the Social Service Bureau, several former welfare workers and a former welfare recipient. He said the workers were frustrated and perplexed by a maze of state and federal regulations which govern how the welfare programs must be administered.

"At times no one knows which (rules) should hold forth," he said. The city, he also suggested, might have fewer people on its

welfare rolls if it—not state and federal officials—had established eligibility rules.

Citing figures indicating the city pays more than a fourth of the costs of the local welfare program, Barfield asked for support for his conclusion that the state should handle the entire program and pay all of its costs. The remainder of the costs come from state and federal funds.

"Mr. Barfield," Martin replied smiling, "we have already done that."

"It hasn't been done," Barfield answered.

Martin said the proposal was

in a list of recommendations the council has forwarded to the Hampton Roads Committee for Areawide Cooperation for consideration by area legislators. Maxwell, he said, has also discussed the matter with other city managers in the area.

"What has this to do with this purge?" he asked Barfield. "Was any member of council not aware that Mr. Maxwell was not pursuing this as hard as he can?"

The mayor also told Barfield that the procedures of the area wide committee (of which "I assume you are aware") are

Roy and his council colleague, Sam T. Barfield sparred frequently on substantive issues. This headline from The Virginian-Pilot *of August 19, 1967, pertained to findings of Barfield's investigation of the city's welfare department. Martin accused Barfield of undermining the council's probe into the operation of the agency.*

Jordan's Win Called New Day in Politics

By DON ALLGOOD

NORFOLK — The victory of Joseph A. Jordan Jr. was hailed by many today as the dawning of a new day in Norfolk politics, but it's unlikely to upset the even tenor of Norfolk's city government, administraton l e a d e r s were saying in the wake of the Negro lawyer's election to City Council.

Jordan won despite a concerted effort by the administration of Mayor Roy B. Martin Jr. to keep its incumbent seven-man council "team" together.

Paul Schweitzer, a C o u n c i l member for eight years, was the loser.

Councilman Sam T. Barfield

**Other Election News
On Page 41**

When the long-sought victory finally was certain (he ran for office three times previously), Jordan spoke of relying on persuasion to promote his ideas at City Hall.

He left no doubt as to his intentions of bringing to the office what he feels is some fresh thinking, particularly in regard to the city government's responsiveness to the needs and problems of "the little man."

(Continued on Page 11, Col. 1)

African-American attorney Joseph A. Jordan Jr.'s bid for a city council seat broke Roy Martin's team ticket, unseating Paul Schweitzer, in the 1968 election. Jordan won, despite a concerted effort by Martin to keep his team together. "I can't envision any greater upheaval in the council chamber, unless one member wants it that way." He continued, "We (the incumbents) are six men who basically stand for the same type of government." So said Roy in the June 18, 1968 Ledger-Star, which ran the article, "Jordan's Win Called New Day in Politics."

between Martin and Kellam never improved either.

The election of 1968 was called "a cliff-hanger whose outcome was in doubt almost to the end,"[20] but the stage had been set a week before the election, on June 4, when Martin let it be known he was leading the charge to derail black candidate Joseph A. Jordan Jr.'s candidacy for Norfolk City Council. Roy appealed to friends of the administration to return all three incumbents on the team ticket despite their overwhelming sentiment to place an African American on council. However, two incumbents, William P. Ballard and Sam T. Barfield, had earlier revealed they had considered stepping aside in order to place a black on city council. Jordan, a prominent Civil Rights lawyer and, later, a judge, became the first black to be elected to the council the following week. In a field of eight candidates, including perennial candidate Berry D. Willis Jr., an independent, vying for three incumbent seats, Jordan beat veteran Paul Schweitzer, a member of the administration ticket consisting of Ballard and Barfield. Barfield received the most votes in the election with 13,942, but Jordan came in second with 13,551, followed by Ballard, 13,476.

Schweitzer was trying for a third full term as a councilman, but at sixty-five years of age, was the oldest man in the field. Martin's plea to return qualified incumbent candidates to office, repeated before the polling booths opened, had little effect on white precincts. Jordan picked up the support he needed to win from white polling booths, in addition to a sweep at black precincts citywide. The 1968 election was the first since repeal of the poll tax in Virginia, which significantly increased the black voter pool in Norfolk. In fact, the 28,024 votes cast in the councilmanic election toppled previous voter turnout in the city, a wholly unexpected response to the race for three council seats.

> *"In 1969, Patricia Nixon, the eldest daughter of President Nixon was chosen as the Azalea Festival Queen. She was a delightful young lady and having the President's daughter as the queen added more importance and interest in the festival than usual. I recall that the day of the crowning of the queen, which was a beautiful day in the Norfolk Botanical Garden, I was waiting for the President to arrive as he had agreed to come and crown his daughter. When his car drove up, I met President Nixon and as he put his hand out to shake mine, I told him: "Mr. President, welcome to Norfolk, the Navy capital of the world." Smilingly, he looked at me and said, "Mr. Mayor, when in Norfolk yes, but when in San Diego—no." That was one of the few times I've seen President Nixon have any real humor. He was very gracious during his stay, but immediately after the ceremony, he left to go back to Washington."*—Roy B. Martin Jr.

In July of 1968, yet another major change occurred, one that ended the secret meetings of city council with the manager each Monday. In a 5 to 2 vote, the Norfolk City Council begrudgingly voted to abide by Virginia's adoption of the Freedom of Information Act (FOIA), which had taken effect on June 28. Under the new law, it became illegal for city council to meet in closed session unless the subjects to be discussed included land acquisition, personnel matters, and staff briefings. "I'm very tired of being accused by editorial writers of the local press that this council is dishonest and that this council is breaking the law of the state of Virginia,"[21] Martin said in rebuttal. "These are changing times, and it seems that this is what the people want." He blamed the news media for their rebukes of closed sessions for the council action to abolish secret meetings while also noting that City Attorney Leonard H. Davis had ruled there had been nothing illegal about them in the first place. The Norfolk newspapers of July 30 speculated that the election of Jordan hastened the end of Monday closed sessions perhaps more than any other factor, the standing Virginia law included. Schweitzer's loss also ended an era just as surely as Jordan's began a new one. Schweitzer had been the school board chair during Massive Resistance.

The first break in the Martin ticket, in Roy's view, did not occur until 1970, though there were signs it was coming before that time. Daniel Thornton and Linwood Perkins had chosen not to run for city council in the upcoming election, thus in their place, Martin and his supporters asked Kenneth Perry, a successful businessman instrumental in the development of Ward's Corner, and R. Braxton Hill Jr., an accountant and civic leader, to run for council. Perry lost by a small margin to Stanley Hurst, who had run as an independent. Braxton Hill won. Hurst had no particular agenda or axe to grind, but he did have the endorsement of the police depart-

"*Unquestionably one of the saddest days for me as mayor of the city of Norfolk was in March 1972 when Louise and I had the children skiing at Brice [sic] Mountain. I received a telephone call around seven o'clock in the evening from Pooch Nusbaum, then vice mayor, who told me about Fred Duckworth's murder. Pooch said the mayor's body had been found off Little Creek Road on Major Avenue [near his Algonquin Park home]. Unfortunately, the person who committed this horrible crime has never been identified despite a substantial reward. There were few suspects, but the police department was never able to pin it on any particular individual. As I recall the details, it seemed that Mayor Duckworth used to take this walk every evening at the same time. It was obvious the murder was not for robbery because my understanding is that his coat was buttoned and it didn't seem that there had been any indication of trying to go into his pockets. Fred Duckworth was a very dynamic person. He could be just as tough as anyone or, on the other hand, just as gracious. I've often said that he was the right man at the right time for changing the city of Norfolk from what it had been during World War II into a major metropolitan city. Fred Duckworth, I think, other than my father, had the most influence on my development, both as a public official and a business person. He gave me the opportunity to serve my city, an opportunity that opened doors for many of the chapters of my life and I will always be indebted to him. He was an excellent mayor, a good church man, and a very good friend.*"

—Roy B. Martin Jr.

ment where his brother worked. When the city council convened to vote for the president of the council, "I did not have Hurst's vote nor that of Joe Jordan," noted Martin. "Stanley, by his vote, became a member of what we called the administrative team." Looking at Hurst's voting record, he seldom opposed the Martin-led council's proposals and supported programs Roy considered beneficial to the Norfolk populace.

The election of 1972, however, was more problematic. Braxton Hill ran against Irvine B. Hill for reelection. Irvine Hill had been a continuous supporter of the city council and Martin through most of Roy's years as mayor, but by the early seventies, Irvine was champing at the bit to get onto council. "When I heard Irvine was interested in running, I asked him if he would hold off for two years since I felt two Hills running could be very confusing. I offered him my support if he delayed, but he would not agree to it." Irvine Hill ran and defeated Braxton Hill, putting another, to Roy's surprise, non-Martin supporter on council.

"The day after the election, I went to call on Irvine in his office to congratulate him. I also wanted to ask him over to City Hall to meet with the manager and me, particularly since we had city programs ongoing with which Irvine needed to be familiar. I felt with his background, he was likely to work along with us as much as possible, but to my great shock, without batting an eye, Irvine said, 'Roy, I'm not going to support you for mayor.' I did not understand why at the time. During the campaign, his election coordinator told some of my people not to worry about Irvine; he was going to work alongside the Martin team." Hill's initial lack of support was as much a personal jolt as a professional one. As Roy put it later, "I had no idea that Irvine would change so rapidly from being a supporter to being one who wanted the mayor's position himself. It was clear to me that I could be in serious trouble serving out my last two years on council as mayor." Martin had announced during his last election—in 1970—that he was not going to run again and that the next four years would be his last. In that period, he had been selected to be first on the advisory board, then as vice president of the U.S. Conference of Mayors. Thus, during his last year, in which he had planned to be mayor of Norfolk, he would serve as president of the most prestigious organization in the country for municipal leaders.

Knowing that Joseph A. Jordan Jr., Stanley Hurst, and Irvine B. Hill would cast negative votes for Roy to continue as mayor, the weight of council could only be swung by Robert Summers, the son of his old friend, Ezra Summers. Although Summers voted with Martin's team consistently in past years, he had since taken a position on council as an independent and not committed himself to Roy, even though he had voted for him as mayor in past council elections. When Irvine Hill found out he could not secure four votes for mayor so easily, he made every effort to convince Summers to accept the mayor's post. Although noncommittal for Martin, Summers told him he would not accept the mayor's seat on council as long as Roy was still in it. In August, Roy received a call from Hurst who stated, unequivocally, that while he did not want Martin as mayor, he intended to put his name up and vote for him anyway since he felt the bickering among city council members are stooped "to complete foolishness." A call from Irvine Hill soon followed, Hill saying he intended to support Martin for mayor as well. The vote on council was 6 to 1 for Martin; Jordan casting the only nay vote.

Martin and Jordan, two councilmen with little in common, again sat side by side at the council table. At the council's reorganization meeting on September 1, aside from the vote cast for Martin as mayor, Jordan was elected on a 4 to 3 vote as vice mayor. One of the negative votes against the lone black councilman was Martin's. The two were oil and water, arguing frequently and Martin further complicating the mix by impressing upon the rest of city council that he did not want Jordan as vice mayor under any circumstances. When asked by Martin to withdraw from running for vice mayor, Jordan flatly refused. Martin was no longer the undisputed power on city council with four independents occupying council seats. Hurst, though he had put Martin's name before council, stated his intention to introduce a proposal that the mayor be elected by popular vote of the citizens rather than by city council. Hurst's suggestion was not a new one. Martin had suggested it years before, but no one followed through with the idea. In order to reconcile his council, Roy remarked that "the terms 'Martin team' or 'independent' should be forgotten. We should be a Norfolk team."[22] Unfortunately, Roy was, for the first time, a mayor on the side of the council minority.

Martin lost control of the council when Irvine Hill was elected to council in the May election over an incumbent loyal to the mayor, thus giving Jordan, Hill, Summers, and Hurst the upper hand over Roy and his allies on council—Pooch Nusbaum, the former vice mayor, and George Hughes. The Goldenrod ballot had come to haunt Martin. The Concerned Citizens of Norfolk, a group long affiliated with Jordan, endorsed Hill and Hurst, who in turn promised to work closely with the black vice mayor on all council matters. The independents on council soon made exacting changes that put an independent-backed member on the school board, replacing a Martin appointee, abolished the residency requirement for city employees, and established one night meeting a month.

In the early days of his reign as mayor, Roy could nearly always count on a unanimous council, but his majority eroded gradually until forcing him into the minority that made him so uncomfortable in his last two years as the city's chief executive, a position he had been returned to only after the majority could not agree on an appropriate successor and vocal public sentiment for Martin tripped Jordan's bid to unseat him. "The Split," as it became known on city council, pitted the politics of the independent council members with remnants of the Martin team. "It's the best free show in town," Roy once quipped to a newspaper reporter. By early January 1973, Councilman Hurst had called for Martin's resignation after a heated session of council and a couple of his colleagues, disillusioned by the constant bickering of the city's elected leadership, considered quitting. On March 28, Roy reiterated that he would not seek another term as the city's mayor nor as a councilman, noting only that if he chose to run for public office again, it would be a state office. "If I run for anything, I'll run for the State Senate," he said. "I hope I have no part in the council election other than to vote." He continued, "I am wholeheartedly committed to supporting George Hughes and Pooch Nusbaum if they decide to run," but within a few months, Nusbaum would announce that he was not a candidate for another term on the council.

Roy Martin was among ten American mayors on a goodwill trip to Israel in mid-December 1970. He and his wife, Louise, made the 6,000-mile, eight-day trip sponsored by the mayor of Jerusalem, the Association of Israel Mayors, and the Israel Ministry of Tourism. Mayors selected to participate in the program were intended to represent a broad cross-section of American society. While on the tour, the Martins took in the culture and history of Tel Aviv, Haifa, Netanya, Jerusalem, and Tiberias. The Martins dined as guests of El Al Israel Airlines at the Fontainebleau Restaurant on Dizengoff Street in Tel Aviv the evening of December 12, 1970.

Chapter 10

Norfolk's Ambassador at Home and Abroad

As a mayor who saw the well-being of his own city intrinsically tied to that of municipalities across the country and around the world, Roy began to become increasingly proactive in national affairs impacting cities. He visited the White House on a number of occasions for bill signings, but at other times, the visits were intended to brief municipal leaders on cutting edge social policy emanating from Washington. President Lyndon Johnson invited the Martins, along with mayors and their spouses from other cities, to the White House for dinner in the winter of 1965. Johnson, who had begun the hard push for the Great Society, his package of social reform legislation, to Congress that January was itching to get a reaction from a select group of city leaders. "This was a most interesting evening because after a cocktail, the president turned to the First Lady and said, 'Lady Bird, take the ladies up and show them around our living quarters. I want to talk to the mayors.'" Johnson invited the mayors to another room, where members of his cabinet lay in wait to sell the mayors on the finer points of the Great Society program. Martin's one question pertained to a pay bill making its way through Congress. He wanted to know if it might pass. "Secretary of Defense Robert McNamara was speaking and I asked him if the bill would be enacted. Before he could respond, President Johnson turned around, first looking at me and then Secretary McNamara, then he said: 'Don't you answer that question until we get an answer from Senator [Harry Flood Jr. (1965–1983)] Byrd.'" The answer was not forthcoming, namely because it entailed a pay bill which, if passed, stood to provide pay increases for the military. Not that a pay increase to the military was out of line, but Johnson's advisors cautioned against competitive legislation that stood to siphon off funding to Great Society programs and the primary defense budget, then focused almost entirely on the escalating war in Southeast Asia.

During the Azalea Festival in Norfolk that April, President Johnson came to the city for the crowning of his daughter, Luci Baines Johnson, as Queen Azalea XII. "The next time I was at the White House after the festival for a bill signing, I went up to the podium to receive the pen that President Johnson had just used and as I turned to walk away, he called to me and said, 'Mayor, come back. I want to ask you how the azaleas are getting along.' I was pleased he remembered."

In 1968, Roy Martin was elected president of the Virginia Municipal League, which he had served over the years in various capacities. As a legislative body, the league maintained considerable influence with the General Assembly. Martin's

While president of the Virginia Municipal League, Roy and Louise Martin hosted one of many dinners and receptions for the state's local officials. Here, the mayor of Roanoke engages Louise and Virginia Governor Mills E. Godwin in conversation as Martin looks on. The photograph is circa 1968. (Buddy Norris, photographer.)

involvement with the Virginia Municipal League unquestionably led him to serve on many committees, including the executive committee of the National League of Cities, an association that was heavily supported by municipal leagues around the country.

On September 16, 1971, while Roy served as chairman of the national advisory board of the U.S. Conference of Mayors, he had the opportunity, along with then Conference president Henry W. Maier, mayor of Milwaukee, and Mayor Louis Welch of Houston, to visit Vice President of United States Spiro T. Agnew.

Queen Azalea XII was Luci Baines Johnson, daughter of President of the United States Lyndon B. Johnson. She is shown here greeting Vice President Humphrey at the luncheon. During Martin's tenure as Norfolk mayor, nothing exposed the area to greater regional cooperation than the Azalea Festival—at least in a friendly sort of way. (Official United States Navy photograph.)

This photograph, taken in the office of the vice president of the United States, on September 16, 1971, shows (left to right) John Gunther (with his back to the camera), then executive director of the United States Conference of Mayors; Roy B. Martin Jr.; Henry W. Maier, mayor of Milwaukee, Wisconsin; Vice President Spiro T. Agnew; and Louis Welch, mayor of Houston, Texas. Maier was president of the U.S. Conference of Mayors at that time. He was succeeded by Louie Welch (1972–73) and Martin (1973–74). (Official White House photograph.)

The issue Martin wanted most to discuss with the vice president—and the issue Agnew was least likely to talk about at that time—was school bussing, a subject particularly relevant to core cities. "I asked if there was any means whereby the federal government could assume part of this cost. Without any hesitation, Agnew offered no encouragement and this subject was immediately dropped." The meeting continued as Martin, joined by Mayors Maier and Welch, urged the vice president to get revenue sharing off the back burner of Congress to help meet the needs not only of cities, but most of the states in the Union. "The vice president's answer was noncommittal. While he was sympathetic to our position, Agnew indicated only that he would look into what could be done to get the legislation moving."

During the series of scheduled meetings in Washington, of which the vice president was one, Martin, Maier, and Welch had a ninety-minute meeting at the White House with President Richard M. Nixon and nine members from the National Governors Association, held in conjunction with the Cost-of-Living Council's report to the president. "We were all pleased to hear the President say that he supported revenue sharing and that he would like to see Congress, in necessary, stay in session until Christmas so they could give the cities and states a very fine Christmas present." However, the question Roy had asked the vice president earlier on the bussing issue, unbeknownst to him, had not been forgotten by the White House.

Nearly three years later, on a return invitation to the White House as president of the U.S. Conference of Mayors, Martin got to the gate of the residence, but his

Roy and Louise Martin pose with then Israeli Minister of Transportation Shimon Peres at the annual Bonds for Israel dinner held on December 19, 1971, in Norfolk. The photograph was forwarded to the Martins by Nat Buchsbaum, who was, at that time, the Virginia and North Carolina area director of State of Israel Bonds, part of the Development Corporation for Israel. Peres was eventually prime minister of Israel from 1984 to 1986 and from 1995 to 1996, and after Yitzhak Rabin's assassination in 1995, he was prime minister, defense minister, and labor party leader but the latter term in office was short-lived. (Courtesy of the State of Israel Bonds.)

During the first week of June 1972, Mayor Martin, accompanied by Louise, visited Norfolk's sister city in Japan—Kitakyushu—on a tour set out by the Kyushu International Cultural Association. As part of the American delegation, the Martins were treated to the best of Japanese culture. In a letter sent June 15, shortly after the Martins' return to Norfolk, Nobuko Yamaguchi, representing the association, remarked that "It was such a wonderful great event in the history of the sister-city program to have two mayors from the United States to a city of Japan. I am reconfirmed that getting to know each other notwithstanding any nationality is the beginning of the human relationship which chains us all over the world. This triple sister-city relationship should give many citizens a limitless and golden opportunity of getting to know [one another], I am sure."

name had been struck from the visitor list. John Gunther, executive director of the Conference, was with him that day. When Gunther heard the problem, he immediately got on the telephone and spoke to Vice President Agnew's staff. Within moments, Martin and Gunther strode up to the White House. The only excuse offered for the snafu was that there were not enough chairs for everyone. "Later, we found out the real reason was that word had leaked to the White House and the Washington media that I was going to bring up the school bussing issue, which I had absolutely no intention of doing. It was amusing when I left the White House," said a bemused Martin, "the number of reporters standing around wanting to know what President Nixon's reaction had been to my remarks about bussing. Much to their disappointment, they found out that there was no such discussion."

"No matter what you might think of a president of the United States—politically or personally," observed Martin, "having the opportunity to visit the White House for a bill signing or a reception was always a real pleasure. It's something you seldom forget." The Martins had been fortunate to attend several bill signing ceremonies with President Johnson, as well as a few by President Nixon. "I still remember my last visit to the White House as mayor of Norfolk," he continued. "That was on August

23, 1974, the month before I retired from city government. I was one of thirty mayors invited by President Gerald R. Ford to the White House for the signing of the housing bill known as the Housing and Community Development Act of 1974." While pleased to be invited, he was not impressed by the legislation. The bill, in its first six years, provided Norfolk about $18 million, but by 1980, the city would get only around $15 million. By comparison, the city received $33 million in 1972. Though Roy had been long retired from public office, he and Louise visited the White House one last time on October 17, 1988, for a luncheon at which Jean Faircloth MacArthur received the Presidential Medal of Freedom from President Ronald Reagan.

With a key federal election on the horizon in November 1972, Martin was appointed head of the Mayors and Municipal Officials for the Re-election of the President by President Richard Nixon. As the announcement was made on August 6, Roy let it be known publicly that he intended to support Democratic U.S. Senator William B. Spong Jr. and Republican Congressman G. William Whitehurst for reelection. Martin, in making his endorsements as chairman of the Virginia committee, affirmed his nonpartisan political stand. He also said that Nixon was the best president for Norfolk and Virginia.

The Norfolk City Council honored Admiral John A. "Jack" McCain Jr., commander in chief of the Pacific, on his retirement, which was official as of September 1, 1972. McCain was appointed commander of United States naval forces in the Pacific on July 31, 1968, shortly after his son, then Navy Lieutenant John S. McCain III, future United States Senator from Arizona, was shot down over North Vietnam and taken prisoner.

Norfolk Mayor Roy B. Martin Jr. shakes hands with President of the United States Richard M. Nixon after the signing of the Revenue Sharing Act on October 20, 1972. This historic ceremony was held at Independence Hall in Philadelphia. Martin was instrumental in seeing the act come to fruition. (Official White House photograph.)

Unquestionably, as Roy's star began to rise on the national scene, especially among prestigious municipal organizations and presidents of the United States, he was able to maneuver an exit from public office that best suited the service he had rendered to the city of Norfolk and to countless associations across the land. "One of the greatest honors that I had in my political and business life was being chosen president of the U.S. Conference of Mayors. The conference is made up of approximately the three hundred largest cities in the United States and, to my knowledge, there was only one mayor from a community the size of Norfolk that was ever honored by being picked to lead this organization. I had the opportunity to meet with and get to know many of the mayors from across America whose names are well-known on the national political scene." Martin hosted the legislative committee of the Conference in Norfolk shortly after becoming president. Members of the committee, which consisted of mayors of major cities, came to Norfolk to observe its redevelopment program. As Martin would later explain, the legislative arm of the Conference met only once or twice annually to observe initiatives in one city, like Norfolk, but have carry-over benefits to communities across the country. The 1973 visit to Norfolk included John Vliet Lindsay, mayor of New York City from 1966 to 1973, Mayor Thomas Bradley, of Los Angeles, who served his constituency from 1973 to 1993, and six additional mayors from large municipalities scattered from coast to coast. Norfolk was decidedly in the spotlight cast by Martin's new position as head of the Conference.

As president of the nation's premier mayoral association, Roy traveled extensively both in the United States and abroad, thus becoming the city's ambassador to far-flung corners of the globe and laying the foundation for many of the enduring relationships in foreign lands enjoyed today by Norfolk's leadership. "Many of

Martin (left) was photographed on the steps of the White House with Mayor Maynard Jackson of Atlanta, Georgia, in August of 1974. Atlanta became the first major city in the South to elect a black mayor—Maynard Jackson—in 1973.

Lawrence E. Spivak, host of "Meet the Press," "America's Press Conference of the Air," took advantage of the U.S. Conference of Mayors event in San Francisco and called over several mayors to take part in a program taped in San Diego on June 23, 1974. Spivak is seated center. His press panel on the left included Robert Novak (seated third at the political commentators' table), now co-host of CNN's "Crossfire," a platform for political debate, and also the network's "Evans, Novak, Hunt & Shields," an interview program. The mayors on the right side of the room include (front row left to right) Martin; Dick Lugar, mayor of Indianapolis, Indiana; and Thomas Bradley, mayor of Los Angeles. The second tier includes (left to right) Abe Beame, of New York City; Maynard Jackson, mayor of Atlanta; and Pete Wilson, then mayor of San Diego. Richard G. "Dick" Lugar was a two-term mayor of Indianapolis who ascended to the U.S. Senate during the administration of President Ronald Reagan and is today a senior Republican in the upper house of Congress. Abraham D. "Abe" Beame, mayor of New York City from 1974 to 1977, was the Big Apple's first Jewish mayor. Pete Wilson was mayor of San Diego from 1971 to 1983, when he was elected to the U.S. Senate as a Republican. He was subsequently governor of California from 1991 to 1999. Thomas "Tom" Bradley was elected mayor of Los Angeles in 1973 after serving a decade on city council. He was Los Angeles' first African-American mayor and was reelected four times, serving until 1993. (Photograph courtesy of "Meet the Press.")

these trips would not have been possible, however, had I not been president of the Conference. For example, I was dispatched to Vienna, Austria, for the World Conference on the Environment. I spent three days attending presentations wearing earphones translating into English the remarks of speaker after speaker from various countries."

In February of 1974, again due to his presidency of the U.S. Conference of Mayors, Martin was invited to speak to the Executive Club of Chicago. The afternoon he arrived at the LaSalle Hotel, Chicago was in the middle of a snowstorm and by the next morning, the streets and sidewalks around the hotel had been blanketed in deep snow. Later that morning, Roy received a call from Chicago Mayor Richard J. Daley (1955–1976), who regretted that due to the impassable conditions in the city, he could not leave City Hall to attend the luncheon at which Martin was to speak. Despite the anticipated absence of Chicago's mayor, then one of the most influential in the country, the club opted to go forth with the luncheon. Though the turnout was small, he proceeded with remarks focused on Congress' lack of response to the plight of American cities, a theme Roy carried through to the U.S. Conference of Mayors annual convention that following June in San Diego. "Dick Daley and I were on the legislative committee of the Conference and it was this group which met during the year to review federal legislation concerning American cities. When our members wanted to divert a funding source to support public programs we were pushing, the typical response was to take dollars from the national defense budget, which was always rather disconcerting for me." On one occasion, Roy must have been unusually vocal in his retort to such a suggestion because Daley cut him off and launched into a series of well-taken points as to why Norfolk's mayor was not adequately backing the Conference leadership's position on funding sources. "That afternoon, when I was back in my hotel room, Dick called me and said he hoped I did not take his remarks personally, noting that if he were mayor of Norfolk, his position would be the same as mine."

The trip that followed to the Union of Soviet Socialist Republics in May 1974, while associated with the Conference of Mayors, was directed through an exchange

During his tenure as president of the United States Conference of Mayors, Martin, in has last year in office, gave a press conference in San Francisco, California, during the June opening of that year's gathering of the nation's mayors. To Martin's left is Moon Landrieu, mayor of New Orleans and president of the conference from 1975 to 1976, and to his right is Joseph L. Alioto, mayor of the city of San Francisco, who was Martin's immediate successor as president of the country's premiere gathering of city leadership. (San Francisco Public Utilities Commission photograph.)

On Sunday, December 13, 1970, the Martins departed Tel Aviv for Netanya, located on the shores of the Mediterranean Sea. Netanya was established in 1928 and is named for the celebrated American philanthropist Nathan Strauss. While in the seaside resort, they visited the Ben Yehuda Absorption Center (Ulpan) to meet recent arrivals to Israel and see firsthand how the young people are taught Hebrew.

program established by President Nixon and President Leonid Brezhnev of the Soviet Union. As president of the Conference, Roy was selected to represent the leadership of American cities. He was accompanied by a delegation which included Louise; John Gunther, executive director of the U.S. Conference of Mayors, and his wife; and the mayor of Fort Worth, then vice president of the Conference, and his spouse. Unfortunately, the Fort Worth mayor had to return home after a couple of days for personal reasons. "We were given what I have always called the 'red carpet treatment,'" recalled Roy fondly of the trip that took him three-quarters of the way around the world. "We first visited Moscow and after the first night there, our Russian hosts took us to the Kremlin for a great performance." But during the performance, the American delegation was called out of the auditorium and put on a train bound for Leningrad. There, they visited for a few days, then went on to

Minsk, an industrial city, and to Odessa, a port city on the Black Sea. The last stop on tour was Moscow, where it had all begun days earlier. During their visit around the republics, Martin and the others got snapshot views of municipal facilities and met briefly with their counterparts in various communities. The last day, while still in Moscow, the Americans signed what the Russians called "great papers of cooperation" in the Kremlin.

As representatives of the United States sponsored by the Department of State, "we had every opportunity to meet with the American ambassador to the Soviet Union as well as consuls to each of the Russian cities that we visited. It was eye open-

The President of Israel, the Honorable Zalman Shazar, received the Martins at his official residence in Jerusalem on December 15, 1970. Shazar, shown shaking hands with Mayor Martin, noted on the occasion of the American mayors' visit that "you will be given the opportunity to see all that interests you—from ancient sites, like those in Jerusalem, in which so many of you are interested, to the new developments which in so many cases owe so much to American help."

ing to experience the feelings of the people of Russia about what they called the great 'patriotic war'—World War II. We visited a number of their monuments and cemeteries. As one might expect for that time in history, we were completely controlled in our activities."

Before visiting the Soviet Union, a good friend of Louise Martin advised her if she wanted to acquire anything particular while in the country or if she had need of something, no matter what it might be, "just talk to the chandelier." On a prior trip to the Soviet Union, the friend and her husband attended an elaborate dinner, but as delightful as the meal had been, it was served with coarse-textured paper napkins. After the couple returned to their hotel room later that evening, Louise's friend commented on the napkin's quality to her husband. The next morning at breakfast, much to her surprise, the woman was furnished with a fine linen napkin. "Louise had wanted to acquire an icon and at that time they were not for sale. While we were in our suite she would laugh softly and say to the chandelier: 'I certainly would like an icon.' Early the morning we were leaving, our escort, a nice young man, appeared at the door with a package that he instructed me to give to Mrs. Martin. It turned out to be a small, but very beautiful, icon."

Perhaps the most eventful moment for Roy, which occurred rather by happenstance at the June annual convention of the nation's mayors, gave him national media exposure he never expected. Ronald Reagan was then governor of California and addressed the Conference, but he was, in later years, more significant for what he later became—president of the United States; he was not the news of the conference in many respects. The nation was immersed in Watergate gossip and the mounting troubles of the president, Richard Nixon, by the time the mayors convened in California. The operation of the federal government—and Congress—had slowed as those in the executive branch faced serious criminal charges. As president of the fraternity of mayors, from his opening remarks at the convention, Roy became a news story of national note. David Broder reported in *The Washington Post* that Martin believed Watergate made it impossible for government to govern, but declared the forecast impeachment and trial of President Nixon disastrous for the nation's cities. "I recommended resignation by the president rather than his impeachment was the answer."

Reflecting over two decades later on twelve years as mayor, one of the most interesting opportunities that came along was an invitation to join nine other mayors and their spouses for a trip to Israel as guests of the Israeli government. "I am confident that my invitation came about because of the strength of the Jewish community in Hampton Roads. We spent ten glorious days in Israel." On the final day, the president of Israel gave a reception. During the event, Louise and Roy were called away to the world headquarters of the United Jewish Appeal, where they were warmly received and presented with a bayonet, one of the first weapons manufactured in Israel. The Martins were the only couple in their exchange group to be so honored.

Aside from globe-trotting Europe, the Soviet Union, Israel, and even Japan, the Martins went on several trips with the Norfolk Port and Industrial Authority and Twenty-first Street Business Association. Each year a consortium from the two organizations left on sponsored cruises from Norfolk to the Caribbean, usually with a Roman Catholic priest, Protestant minister, Jewish rabbi, and an official greeter aboard to smooth relations once reaching the group's island destination. Martin was chosen the first time to lead a junket departing Norfolk on February 1, 1968, for two weeks in the Caribbean islands. But on more than one occasion, he was tapped to be the greeter on the trips as the years wore on, always the city's most enthusiastic booster at home and abroad.

Norfolk Will Always Remember Roy

Testifying before the United States Senate on Banking, Housing and Urban Affairs' Subcommittee on Housing and Urban Affairs on April 10, 1973, Roy Martin spoke eloquently to the infusion of federal funds in Norfolk's redevelopment and housing effort and the roll call of results that made the Title I program such a success in this 300-year-old port city which had become the first municipality in the nation to have an urban renewal program under the Housing Act of 1949. As he extolled the benefits of Title I, Roy summarily listed a roster of Martin-team initiatives brought to fruition under his leadership in the dozen years he was Norfolk's mayor.

As Roy moved to read the roster of Norfolk programs that had benefited from federal money, he remarked that while the U.S. Department of Housing and Urban Development (HUD) could quote Norfolk's experience, "the results are even better."[24] The estimated annual tax receipts to the city from redeveloped land were estimated to have increased some 450 percent, or almost $5 million per year, which did not include land put to public reuse, such as Norfolk's new police headquarters and a precinct house, three fire stations, and ten parking garages. Roy's figures did not include Scope, the city's cultural and convention center, or a new main library and a branch library, both of which had been sorely needed, nor the expansion of Old

This portrait of Mayor Roy B. Martin Jr., taken in the Norfolk City Council chambers on June 8, 1973, was the last formal photograph of him in office. (R. C. Tamburino, photographer. Studio 111.)

When Roy Martin retired as mayor and member of the Norfolk City Council in 1974, former council-man Cy Perkins presented him with a Kenneth Harris watercolor of downtown Norfolk, which featured the new City Hall, constructed while Martin was president of the council.

Dominion University and Norfolk State College (not yet a university), a new board of education building, two elementary schools, one junior high school and two senior high schools, and an impressive public park and recreation center, a public health building and mental health clinic, the Red Cross headquarters, Eastern Virginia Medical School, and four new hospital buildings. Martin's ability to exercise federal funding judiciously had brought tremendous benefits to the city, the Norfolk that had risen like a phoenix from its foundations under Roy's leadership.

Roy oversaw his last Norfolk City Council meeting on August 27, 1974, with humor and grace. "I guess people are expecting me to express some profound or sentimental thought,"[25] he mused as he banged the gavel used to close some six hundred council meetings in his twelve-year tenure as the city's mayor. "In all those years I've only had to ask one person to leave the chamber," Roy quipped, but it also was not as if he had not been tempted to do it more often. "The most interesting opponent through the years was Berry Willis," a trial attorney, he continued. Willis and Martin engaged in bitter exchanges during city council meetings. However, when Roy needed Willis' support to remain mayor in 1972, Willis readily offered it. The most humorous encounters belonged to a fellow named "Hardtimes Hunt," now deceased sage of Oyster, Virginia, who repeatedly visited Norfolk City Council with a plan to merge the metropolis of Norfolk with the sleepy hamlet on the Eastern Shore. But Hardtimes Hunt had his competition in the humor category. Unlike many of his predecessors—and some of his successors—Roy never had an unlisted telephone number, which he readily admitted of late often made for interesting thirteenth-hour calls. "I once got a call from a sailor in Australia looking for his girlfriend in Norfolk," Martin told reporter Don Hunt of *The Pilot*. He never did find the young lady in question.

With his departure from city council, Norfolk was left for the first time since World War II, without a strong mayor—and powerful voice. The election of 1974 produced a crop of new faces that differed radically from the Duckworth era and Martin years. The new governing body of the city of Norfolk included two former police officers, a woman—the city council's first—with a populist political slant, a prominent physician, a black attorney, and an insurance executive and political loner. The mayor-select, Irvine B. Hill, while a businessman, came from a nontraditional business medium: radio and country and western music. A string of independents made up the new council: R. Stanley Hurst, Claude J. Staylor Jr., Betty Ann Howell, Dr. Mason Cooke Andrews, Vice Mayor Joseph A. Jordan Jr., Robert E. Summers, and, of course, the city's new chief executive—Hill.

The new council, sworn in on September 3, differed in their cohesiveness—or lack thereof—trying hard in many respects to run from what Brown Carpenter, then *Ledger-Star* political reporter, called a council "long dominated by successful businessmen with old family ties."[26] Previous councils had often been accused of being what Carpenter dubbed "closed corporations with plutocratic bent." Hill, as the city's new mayor, vowed not to become the strong mayor that his predecessors had been for nearly a quarter century. The new council was not going to take direction on issues from him. Not surprisingly, Roy was as gracious to Irvine Hill as he passed the mantle of leadership as he had felt compelled to do when Hill, as a new councilman two years earlier, had vowed not to support Martin for a sixth term as president of the council (though Hill eventually supported him). Roy called to wish Hill his warmest congratulations on gaining the votes on council to be elected mayor. And he meant it. "He offered to help me all he could in the transition and was extremely kind," Hill was widely quoted as saying at the time. "I am strongly opposed to a strong-mayor form of government, such as we have had in the past,"[27] said R. Stanley Hurst. Hill concurred with Hurst. "I would be interested in an interacting council and citizen input," Hill remarked, affirming his colleagues statement.

Within six months of Roy's retirement from city council, City Manager G. Robert House was forced to resign his position. Of the resignation, Martin said: "The so-called independence of council is no longer there. It's very obvious it's the Hill administration, or better called the Hurst administration,"[28] referring to the council's acceptance—without discussion—of House's letter on a 5 to 2 vote. Only Councilmen Mason Andrews and Summers voted no to letting House be fired. M. Lee Payne, then president of the Norfolk Chamber of Commerce, noting the atmosphere in the city, said that the council had been what he called "drifting." Payne also remarked that "there was a lack of positive direction," citing "the 180-degree turnaround with a leaderless, vacillating group. Let's get to positive leadership and to a progressive course of action."[29]

A *Ledger-Star* editorial on February 12, 1975, had already fired a pointed verbal salvo at Mayor Hill and the council. "It is hard to decide which is worse in the Norfolk City Council's firing of City Manager House: the loss of an unusually talented municipal administrator or the way in which the council went about getting rid of him." Councilman Mason Andrews, who had voted against House's ouster, added: "I am seriously concerned about the quality of local government.

Judgments may differ," continued Andrews, "from time to time, but they must be made openly and properly if the risk of serious error and suspicion of improper pressure or motivation is to be avoided."

The city council as Roy left it, had become so fragmented, little was accomplished under Mayor Hill's time in office. In an interview in *New Norfolk*'s July–August issue in 1974, published shortly before Roy was to leave the mayor's office for the last time, he told the interviewer that he did not believe the council wanted a strong mayor in office anymore. "A strong personality may come along, but it will not be a strong mayor—one who can lead council decisions." Roy also did not feel confident there would come a time when a mayor could serve as many consecutive terms as he and his predecessor, Fred Duckworth, had done. Hill's twenty-two-month term as mayor from September 3, 1974, to June 30, 1976, seemed to bear out Martin's point. Hill lost his seat on city council in the 1976 election, as did Hurst, succumbing to Vincent J. Thomas, who was elected mayor at the council's subsequent reorganizational meeting, and to Conoly Phillips, a councilman who went on to serve for over a quarter century.

While the Martin years endured the brunt of criticism—as did their namesake from time to time—on the record, the team that Roy Martin assembled, himself included, deserved better. "Theirs has been in many ways a spectacular stewardship,"[30] wrote an editorialist a few months before the Martin years gave way to a new regime on the Norfolk political horizon. Most often criticized for neglecting people in favor of bricks and mortar "is nonsense," said *The Virginian-Pilot*, which like its sister newspaper, *The Ledger-Star*, had both criticized and praised Martin's leadership for over two decades.

> *Whatever the difficulties in the planning, building and operation of Scope, just one example, this was a bold undertaking that has produced a facility affording the people untold entertainment opportunities. The medical complex has helped bring about improved treatment for thousands of people. Adoption of a local sales tax in 1964 was a courageous, progressive tax designed to provide quality education for Norfolk schoolchildren, well before the state started talking seriously about it. Bringing the Walter Chrysler art collection here already has yielded great enjoyment and enrichment for thousands of people. The efforts [of this team]—for so long successful—to keep from raising the real estate tax meant a tangible benefit to many elderly and other homeowners of modest means.*

Ultimately, it was near to impossible to count the number of jobs created for people by all the bricks-and-mortar changes the Martin years heaped upon the city. The Martin-led city council held out against what were tough times for America's core cities. Terms heard little today unless in the pages of a history book—white

COSMOPOLITAN CLUB OF NORFOLK
PRESENTATION CEREMONIES
IN HONOR OF

THE HONORABLE ROY B. MARTIN, JR.

For Distinguished Service as Norfolk's First Citizen
in Civic Affairs for the Year 1973
LAFAYETTE YACHT CLUB
NORFOLK, VIRGINIA

Friday Evening, January 25th, 1974
AT 6:30 P.M.

Roy was honored as Norfolk's First Citizen for 1973 by the Cosmopolitan Club of Norfolk. A dinner was held in his honor on January 25, 1974, at the Lafayette Yacht Club.

flight, segregation, cross-town bussing, and downtown commercial decline—were pervasive ones when Martin was first appointed to city council, but many of them had receded or gone completely by the time he left.

The Martin administration's Achilles' heel was, as one city official it so well, "it didn't want to give anyone else a seat at the table. By design or by accident, the public impression grew that whatever the issue was, it would be handled the Martin way and by the Martin people."[31] There was no room for diverse points of view, and like his predecessor, Fred Duckworth, Roy did not tolerate disagreement well. As the Martin team weakened, Roy was never the peacemaker or apologist, but kept on the course his internal compass told him was the right one for Norfolk. Linwood Perkins, Roy's longtime vice mayor, has said, "Roy never tried to dictate anything. He was always honest and straightforward. He always let us make our own decisions."[32] Vincent J. Thomas, a close friend of Martin and former Norfolk mayor himself, commented on the loss of closed-session council meetings, saying "They just tried to come to some consensus,"[33] before going into very public city council sessions.

Despite his often sharp rebukes of critics and colleagues, Roy was an articulate spokesman for the financial

Roy Martin enjoys a lighthearted moment with Mayor Moon Landrieu of New Orleans and Vice President of the United States Gerald R. Ford (seated right) at a January 1974 meeting of the U.S. Conference of Mayors held in Washington, D.C. Martin was president of the Conference of Mayors at that time.

plight of cities, gaining what some observed as national prestige and regard among his fellow mayors, which was most noticeable in his election as president of the U.S. Conference of Mayors. "The irony of his election," wrote an editor for *The Virginian-Pilot* on May 5, 1974, "is that he stood a fair chance of being ousted from office at home even as he prepared to take the helm of the national office." The candor for which he was so well known could often be to his detriment, sometimes turning to complete inappropriateness. When awarded the Cosmopolitan Club of Norfolk's First Citizen accolade for 1973, Roy turned his acceptance

The Martins posed with former President of the United States George H. Bush and First Lady Barbara Bush (left) and United States Senator John Warner of Virginia during the Bushes visit to the MacArthur Memorial in October 1996.

speech into a political address that called for the retention of the businessman's government and recommending election restrictions to control the activities he did not like. He simply resented "the implication that anyone worked harder at area-wide cooperation than he did,"[34] thus his clashes with Virginia Beach political boss Sidney Kellam, whose own ego and desire to control a piece of the regional pie also got in the way of broader metropolitan collaboration.

When remembering Roy Martin, it is the total effort that must be taken into account, thinking instead of his unselfishness, the competence, vitality, and shoot-from-the-hip honesty that defined him as a leader. It translated into spectacular growth and improvement for the city. He was, however, "the last of a breed," that gave cities such as Norfolk a roadmap for success that could not have been forged prior to World War II. As he left public office for good on August 31, 1974, Roy penned an open letter to the people of Norfolk in which he said: "There is still much to be done, so let us not lose our momentum or desire for progress. The new Norfolk was not brought about by discord, but through cooperation and dedication to service by those elected to serve as its council. Our opportunities are still great; let us not see them pass by." Indeed, Norfolk, let no opportunity pass by and when you grab hold of one, think of the mayor of nearly a quarter century ago who left his chair in the mayor's office and, with it, his behest that those taking his place take care of the city he so loved and which will always remember Roy.

Roy Martin (left) was photographed with Norfolk Mayor Joseph A. Leafe and First Lady Barbara Bush on June 15, 1990. The First Lady attended a ceremony at the MacArthur Memorial at which Jean MacArthur, General Douglas MacArthur's widow was also present. (Official White House photograph.)

ENDNOTES

[1] *The Ledger-Star,* April 15, 1974.

[2] *Ibid.*

[3] "The Martin Years," *The Virginian-Pilot,* August 5, 1974.

[4] *The Virginian-Pilot,* March 28, 1961.

[5] *The Ledger-Star,* June 1, 1961.

[6] *The Virginian-Pilot,* November 2, 1966.

[7] *The Ledger-Star,* September 1, 1966.

[8] September 1, 1966.

[9] Cammy Sessa, "Museum Wing Set for Takeoff," *The Virginian-Pilot,* November 30, 1967.

[10] George H. Tucker, "Godwin Praises Museum," *The Virginian-Pilot,* November 30, 1967.

[11] Staige D. Blackford, "Medical Center Expansion Approved," *The Virginian-Pilot,* October 12, 1966.

[12] *Ibid.*

[13] *Ibid.*

[14] Don Hunt, *The Virginian-Pilot,* August 18, 1974.

[15] *The Ledger-Star,* September 1, 1966.

[16] *Ibid.*

[17] *Ibid.*

[18] Bill McAllister, "Martin Urges Talks to Merge Norfolk and Virginia Beach," *The Virginian-Pilot,* June 14, 1967.

[19] *Ibid.*

[20] Staige D. Blackford, "2 Portsmouth Negroes, 1 in Norfolk Win," *The Virginian-Pilot,* June 12, 1968.

[21] *The Virginian-Pilot,* July 24, 1968.

[22] Gary Dalton, "Martin Mayor Again, Jordan Vice Mayor," *The Virginian-Pilot,* September 2, 1972.

[23] Brown Carpenter, "Martin repeats vow not to run," *The Ledger-Star,* March 29, 1973.

[24] *Congressional Record,* Volume 119, No. 57, April 11, 1973, pp. S7100.

[25] Don Hunt, *The Virginian-Pilot,* August 28, 1974.

[26] August 3, 1974.

[27] Don Hunt, *The Virginian-Pilot,* August 2, 1974.

[28] *The Virginian-Pilot,* February 10, 1975.

[29] *Ibid.*

[30] Editorial, *The Virginian-Pilot,* May 4, 1974.

[31] *Ibid.*

[32] Don Hunt, "Norfolk Will Remember Roy," *The Virginian-Pilot,* August 18, 1974.

[33] *Ibid.*

[34] Editorial, *The Virginian-Pilot,* May 4, 1974.

SUGGESTED READING

While the prologue covers the sources used to craft Roy Martin's biography—and consequently the bibliography—a suggested reading list is provided. For more history of Norfolk and Virginia Beach, including vignettes and stories pertaining to the people and places that have shaped the region, the author has written several books which are highly recommended, including *Mighty Oaks From Little Acorns Grow: The History of Norfolk Collegiate School* (Hallmark Publishing, 2000); *The Jamestown Exposition: American Imperialism on Parade, Volumes I and II* (Arcadia, 1999); *Norfolk's Church Street: Between Memory and Reality* (Arcadia, 1999); *Ocean View* (Arcadia, 1998); *Summer on the Southside* (Arcadia, 1998); *Virginia Beach: Jewel Resort of the Atlantic* (Arcadia, 1998); *Winter Comes to Norfolk* (Arcadia, 1997); and *Norfolk, Virginia: The Sunrise City by the Sea* (Donning, 1994). The author has an extensive list of published and forthcoming titles, of which these are but a few.

Books of local interest on the author's list of favorites include Stephen S. Mansfield's *Princess Anne County and Virginia Beach* (Donning, 1989, 1991) and W. Hugh Moomaw's *Virginia's Belt Line Railroad: The Norfolk & Portsmouth* (Hallmark, 1998). Mansfield and Moomaw have written their respective subjects with a keen eye for detail and accuracy, traits that are all-important in crafting historical text. Finally, anything by George Holbert Tucker is a treat because George knows how to tell a good story.

INDEX

About the Author

Amy Waters Yarsinske, a Hampton Roads native, received her bachelor of arts degrees in economics and English from Randolph-Macon Woman's College and master of planning degree from the University of Virginia School of Architecture. She is a well-known and respected author and journalist, whose publishing interests run the gamut of regional and national history, historical biography, military and aviation history, and nonfiction subject matter. Though her professional and community affiliations are extensive, Amy is a past president of the Norfolk Historical Society and the Norfolk Historical Foundation, a member of the Rotary Club of Norfolk, the Association of Naval Aviation and its Hampton Roads Squadron, the Naval Order of the United States and the organization's Hampton Roads Commandery, and a 1998 alumnus of the prestigious CIVIC Leadership Institute. She is a member of Washington Independent Writers, the Authors Guild, and a recent inductee into the Virginia Center for the Book's distinguished Virginia Authors Room. She is the author of many books, among them, *From Hellcats to Tomcats—and the Sting of the Hornet: The History of Naval Air Station Oceana* (Hallmark Publishing, 2001); "Memories and Memorials" in *Naval Aviation* (Hugh Lauter Levin Associates, 2001); *Forward for Freedom: The Story of Battleship Wisconsin* (BB-64) (The Donning Company/Publishers, 2001); *The Jamestown Exposition: American Imperialism on Parade, Volumes I and II* (Arcadia, 1999); and *Wings of Valor, Wings of Gold: An Illustrated History of U.S. Naval Aviation* (Flying Machines Press, 1998). She and her husband, Raymond, reside in Norfolk with their three children.